THE HIGHLAND SCOTS
OF NORTH CAROLINA
1732-1776

THE HIGHLAND SCOTS
OF NORTH CAROLINA
1732-1776

by

DUANE MEYER

Chapel Hill
THE UNIVERSITY OF NORTH CAROLINA PRESS

Manufactured in the United States of America
ISBN-13: 978-0-8078-0829-0
ISBN-10: 0-8078-0829-6
ISBN-13: 978-0-8078-4199-0 (pbk.)
ISBN-10: 0-8078-4199-4 (pbk.)

10 09 08 07 06   16 15 14 13 12

To

LYN

Proverbs 31 : 10

PREFACE

While studying eighteenth-century Europe at the State University of Iowa a decade ago, I prepared a paper on what is known as the Forty-five, the Jacobite rebellion in Scotland in the year 1745. The research involved in this project revealed a discrepancy between American and British interpretations of the reasons for the emigration of Highlanders to America in the eighteenth century. This discrepancy proved to be an irresistible challenge to investigation. The response to the challenge brought into focus an intriguing paradox that long has puzzled the students of American history: why did the Highlanders, bitter foes of the House of Hanover in the first half of the eighteenth century, rally to the unpopular cause of George III thirty years after their defeat and humiliation in the Forty-five? A dissertation emerged from the consideration of the puzzle. That dissertation and the revisions and additions evolving from five years of further research comprise *The Highland Scots of North Carolina, 1732-1776.*

Colonial documents are not consistent in the spelling of Highlander names. For example, Alexander McAlister at various times is referred to as MacAlister, McAlester, McAllister, or McCallister. Land grant records mention several families named Buea who received plots from the crown, but all later references to them spell the name Buie. To bring some order to this orthographic chaos, I have used the spellings which appear most frequently in the original sources.

A writer never works alone. My debts of gratitude are manifold:

to Professor Charles Gibson, of the State University of Iowa, an inspiring scholar and a gracious gentleman, my profound appreciation for years of wise counsel and patient guidance;

to Secretary of State Thad Eure and his staff, of Raleigh, North Carolina, to the staff at the North Carolina Archives in Raleigh, and to the staffs of the University of North Carolina Library and the Southern Historical Collection at Chapel Hill, my thanks for their courteous and competent assistance;

to Professor Donald H. Nicholson, Chairman of the Department of History of Southwest Missouri State College, a sage captain, my appreciation for his encouragement;

to Mr. Robert Harvey, Miss Margaret Crighton, Mrs. Marilouise Herd, Miss Billie Hearst, and the staff of the Southwest Missouri State College Library, my gratitude for their kind co-operation;

to Professor Orin Robinson, Mr. James Lawson, and Mr. Robert Good, of Southwest Missouri State College, my thanks for the drawing of the maps and graphs;

to my wife, Marilyn Hansen Meyer, for her interest and encouragement and for her assistance in preparing the maps and charts and in proofing and indexing, my deep appreciation;

to my children, Paul Christian, Mark Lincoln, James Stephen, and Andrea Lynn, for the several hikes and stories they have forfeited, my apologies and my promise to repay every hour.

Duane Meyer

Springfield, Missouri
January 27, 1961

CONTENTS

MAPS AND FIGURES

THE HIGHLAND SCOTS
OF NORTH CAROLINA
1732-1776

CHAPTER I

REVOLUTION AND AFTERMATH

Did you ever hear of a loyal Scot
Who was never concern'd in any plot?
—from *Ancient Ballads of Scotland.*[1]

THE MIGRATION of the Scottish Highlanders to North Carolina began in the 1730's and slowly gained momentum. On the eve of the American Revolution, such large numbers were leaving the Highlands that Samuel Johnson, visiting in North Britain, could speak of an "epidemick desire of wandering which spreads its contagion from valley to valley."[2] The migration brought to America, above all to North Carolina, a large body of settlers known chiefly in American revolutionary history for their devotion to the cause of George III. What can account for the curious transformation of the Highlanders, who in Europe had rallied round the Stuart flag in the Jacobite uprisings known as the Fifteen and the Forty-five, in memory of the years of their occurrence, but who in North Carolina were the loyal supporters of the House of Hanover? Professor Thomas J. Wertenbaker writes: "American historians have been at a loss to explain the loyalty of the Highlanders to the royal cause during the American Revolution. Since many had fought and suffered for the Pretender, and almost all were victims of the recent changes in Scotland for which the government was responsible, one might suppose they would have welcomed an opportunity for revenge."[3]   It is only a little less remarkable that a people so imbued with a love of chief and clan and so attached to the braes and glens of the Highlands should have emigrated at all.

The Highlands of Scotland include those mainland and island areas north and west of a line formed approximately by the foothills of the Grampian Mountains. (See Map I.)   This line begins on the north coast midway between the Nairn River and the Findhorn River and runs south-southeast to include in the Highlands the western tips of the present-day shires of Moray, Banff, Aberdeen, and Angus.   In the shire of Angus it turns southwest to cross Perthshire and finally ends at the Firth of Clyde in Dumbartonshire after passing just south of Loch Lomond. An ethnic distinction may also be made between the Highlanders and the Lowlanders.   The Highlanders were mostly descended from the Irish Gaels while the Lowlanders were the offspring of the Angles of Northumberland.[4]

In the first half of the eighteenth century, the Highlanders lived in a secluded feudal society under the control of tribal chieftains.   A clan warrior received his plot of land from his chief, with whom he usually could claim some blood relationship.   In return, the warrior was expected to attend the court of the chief, accept his justice, follow him in war, and pay him rent in kind.   In this society methods of agriculture were primitive and farming unproductive.   To eighteenth-century Englishmen and Lowlanders, the Highlands seemed a mysterious area populated by people speaking an ancient tongue, perpetuating strange practices, and paying little if any heed to the pronouncements of Parliament.[5]

Captain Edward Burt, an English engineer traveling

MAP I. THE HIGHLANDS AND ISLANDS OF NORTH BRITAIN

through the Highlands in 1730, expressed in his *Letters* his amazement at the society he discovered. The power of the clan chief over his clansmen was almost unlimited. When Burt was offended by the remarks of a chief's warriors, the angered patriarch offered to send him "two or three of their Heads" in apology.[6] A chief never ventured from his castle without a retinue of gillies (servants), a bard, a piper, and a bladier (spokesman). Women performed much of the agricultural labor, using crude implements constructed largely of wood. The horse collar was not yet used in the Highlands; Burt observed that the people maintained the "barbarous Custom . . . of drawing the Harrow by the Horse's Dock, without any manner of harness whatever."[7] Their agriculture barely produced enough in good years to sustain men and cattle. In bad years large numbers of both perished from starvation.[8] Oatmeal, sometimes mixed with a small quantity of milk, at other times with blood from a freshly-bled cow, was the staple food. Butter and eggs were eaten occasionally; meat was consumed rarely.[9] After a sojourn in one of the "wretched hovels" of "piled stone and turf" which served as a home, Burt described the interior in this way: "There my Landlady sat, with a Parcel of Children about her, some quite, and others almost naked, by a little Peat Fire, in the Middle of the Hut; and over the Fire-Place was a small Hole in the Roof for a Chimney. The Floor was common Earth, very uneven, and no where Dry, but near the Fire and in the Corners, where no Foot had carried the Muddy Dirt from without Doors."[10]

The isolation and tribal character of this poverty-stricken society were destroyed in the Jacobite struggle for the throne of England and Scotland. Some account of the political developments born of this conflict is necessary in order to understand the subsequent emigration of many of the clansmen to America. Members of the House of Stuart (also spelled Stewart and Steuart) had occupied the Scottish throne since the year 1316. In England, the Tudors were the ruling family until the line ran out with the death of the Virgin Queen, Elizabeth I, in 1603. Elizabeth's cousin and the Scottish King, James VI, was then invited to accept the English crown also. He did so and ruled England as James I. The two nations retained their separate parliaments and councils, but the people were all subjects of the same Stuart monarchs. James and the Stuarts who succeeded him ruled the two nations for a century altogether. James I (VI) ruled from 1603 to 1625, Charles I from 1625 to 1649, Charles II from 1660 to 1685, James II from 1685 to 1688, Mary Stuart and her husband William of Orange, who were joint sovereigns, from 1689 to 1702, and Anne from 1702 to 1714.

The Stuarts, especially those who reigned before 1688, were strong-willed sovereigns, ever upholding the divine right of kings. James I, who was called "the wisest fool in Christendom" by the Duke of Sully, assumed the role of essayist in order to defend this divine right theory.[11] On the continent, where every state was subject to invasion, strong rulers and state unity were so necessary for protection that the nobility and middle class were frequently willing to forgo political power. But the English and the Scots felt relatively secure behind their ocean moat. They were not fond of arbitrary rule, and they were particularly jealous of the prerogatives of their respective parliaments. When James VI was five years old, having already served as king for three years, he was taken to visit the Scottish Parliament. Bored with the proceedings, he amused himself by poking his finger through a hole in the tablecloth. So occupied, he inquired where he was. When one of the nobles explained that they were in Parliament, the boy king said, "This Parliament has a hole in it."[12] Perhaps this tale is symbolic of what became a conscious Stuart policy of seeking out the flaws and weaknesses in the parliamentary structure. They objected to parliamentary control over the passage of laws and the levying of taxes. In order to minimize parliamentary criticism of the crown for the assessment of illegal taxes and the issuance of illegal laws, parliaments were called as infrequently as possible.[13]

Religion was another source of conflict. James I and Charles I both disliked Calvinist policy, which put church control in the hands of presbyteries and a General Assembly. They preferred to have royally appointed bishops directing the church, and their attempts to establish such an episcopal system in Scotland produced bitter Presbyterian opposition. Charles II was secretly Catholic, but James II openly proclaimed his Catholicism. Wily Charles II moved secretly and slowly toward a policy of toleration for Catholics, but blunt and vigorous James II openly attempted to restore Catholicism to its former place in England and Scotland.[14]

The hostile response of the English and Scottish peoples to these political and religious policies produced some of the most important events in their history. James I and Charles II stirred up a storm of protest by their actions, but they were able to ride out the gale. Charles I and James II were not so fortunate. After a Civil War developed in both Scotland and England, Charles I was made a prisoner of the Puritans and condemned by Puritan justice as "a tyrant, a traitor, murderer, and public enemy of the good people of this nation."[15] He lost his head to the executioner's axe.

James II retained his handsome head, but not his throne. Blunt, relentless man that he was, he pursued his political and religious policies with such harshness and obstinacy that he soon alienated the members of the English and Scottish Parliaments, the Anglicans, and the Calvinists. In view of his advancing years and the Protestantism of the grown daughters who would succeed him, no attempt was made to depose James II until his bride gave birth to a son in 1688. This brought forth the threat of a Catholic succession and triggered the Glorious Revolution of 1688. A coalition of political leaders advised James to leave the country and invited James's daughter Mary and her husband William to become the joint monarchs of England and Scotland. Recalling his father's fate, James fled to France.[16]

Three important developments occurred near the turn of the century. In 1701, the Act of Settlement provided that the monarch must be Protestant. This was obviously intended to disqualify James II and his son. The Act of Union of 1707 unified the two kingdoms of England and Scotland into one new state known as Great Britain, with a single Parliament located at London. The Presbyterian communion was recognized as the established church in Scotland. When Queen Anne died in 1714, the Elector of Hanover became the English king and took the name George I.[17]

After 1688, those people in England and Scotland who favored the restoration of James II or, after his death in 1701, the restoration of his son "James III" were known as Jacobites (from *Jacobus,* the Latin for James). Although they took part in several other uprisings, the main revolutionary efforts of the Jacobites took place in 1715 and 1745 and were, as we have seen, subsequently known as the Fifteen and the Forty-five. It would be naïve to assume the Jacobites were motivated solely by their love for James II or "James III" or the House of Stuart. A great tangle of causes lay behind the attempts to depose the Hanoverians. Some opportunists, having failed to secure places of influence or authority in the Hanoverian government, believed they would have more success after a change of dynasty. British Catholics had an obvious reason for supporting the Jacobite cause. The Episcopalians of North Scotland, who disliked the established Presbyterian Church, recalled that the Stuarts had appointed bishops for Scotland, and they longed for a return to that arrangement. During the first half of the eighteenth century, there was always a sizable group of nonjuring Episcopalian clergymen in Scotland who refused to take an oath of loyalty to the House of Hanover. There were also Jacobites who objected to the Act of Union, which they thought subordinated the welfare of Scotland to that of England. They hoped a revolution might reinstate the separate governments. In the Highlands, there was intense hatred for the Campbells and the Duke of Argyle, who were symbols of Hanoverian power in that area. Fired by this enmity, many clans awaited an opportunity to secure revenge for the humiliations they had suffered under the Campbells.[18]

The Fifteen and the Forty-five were organized in the Highlands of Scotland because there were disgruntled groups in the area and because it was a remote region largely uncontrolled and unpatrolled by the British army. In September, 1715, the Earl of Mar, unhappy at having been removed from his post as Secretary of State by George I, traveled to the Highlands and raised the standard for James Edward, the self-styled "James III."

Two months later, Mar and his army were defeated at Sheriffmuir by a royal force under the command of Archibald Campbell, the third Duke of Argyle.[19] By the time James arrived in Scotland, the tide of battle had turned against his followers. The Episcopal clergy of Aberdeen were delighted with his presence and spoke of him as a new Moses, Joseph, or David.[20] But his military leaders did not share the clergy's pleasure and praise, since James failed to inspire Scotsmen to rally to their dying cause. James remained with his troops for six weeks and then fled to the safety of a ship bound for France. On departing, he left his troops a farewell letter defending his desertion as necessary to secure "a more happy juncture for our mutual delivery."[21] James never returned. He moved to the safety of Italy and the comfort of a yearly 30,000-crown allowance from the Vatican.[22]

The next major Jacobite revolutionary attempt, the Forty-five, was the work of James's son Charles Edward— affectionately known in the Highlands as Bonnie Prince Charlie. Even after the offer of a French army had been withdrawn, the twenty-four-year-old Charles, against the advice of all his associates, sailed for the Highlands in 1745 and debarked to begin his revolutionary adventure with only seven companions.[23] The clan chiefs, recalling the events of 1715 and realizing that foreign assistance was unlikely in a new revolutionary attempt, were displeased when his arrival was announced. Macdonald of Boisdale was the first chief to meet the high-spirited young prince. He advised Charles to go home. The young Stuart retorted, "I am come home, Sir," and refused to be dissuaded from his project.[24] While James had been languid, aloof, and uninspiring, his son was quite the opposite. Charles commanded the admiration and confidence of the Highlanders. He was a tall, slender man with red hair, dark eyes, and a handsome face. Energetic, glib, and ingenuous, he worked hard to make many friends.[25]   Later his life was ruined when he became a bloated, useless drunkard, but in the Forty-five he consumed a bottle of brandy a day "without being in the least concerned."[26]   Charles's Catholicism constituted a serious handicap, since the Lowlanders, as well as many of the Highlanders, were Presbyterian.   He vetoed the many suggestions that he change his religion in order to secure the support of the Lowlanders.[27]   But in spite of great handicaps, the impact of his personality was such that almost half of the clans agreed to rise and follow his standard.[28]

The military prowess of the Highlanders was widely respected, although their tactics seemed primitive and disorganized in comparison with those of other European armies.   The signal to attack was followed by a mad charge at the enemy as the clansmen shrieked, screamed, and brandished their claymores.   The very sound and fury of a Highland army often terrorized its opposition. Prince Charles adopted the Highland garb as his uniform.   At night he wrapped himself in his plaid and slept in the heather with his troops.   Trusting Prince Charles, the Gaels performed mightily for him on the field of battle.

The military campaigns of the Forty-five occurred over an eight-month period and brought terror to George II and his court.   After first rallying the clans at Moidart, Charles marched them out of the Highlands to seize the city of Perth.   He forced the inhabitants of Perth to contribute £500 and then moved his army on south to Edinburgh.   The Hanoverians lacked sufficient troops to halt the invasion, and Edinburgh fell into hands of the Jacobite host without costing them a man.   Charles moved into Holyrood Palace, the ancestral Stuart castle, and proclaimed his father—who was safely ensconced in Italy—James VIII, King of Scotland. Immediately, Sir John Cope and his army approached the capital. Prince Charles led his Gaels out to Prestonpans for the battle. The two armies were of equal size, but Cope's force had the advantage in artillery and dragoons. When the Highlanders opened the encounter with a furious rush and a blaze of fire, the Hanoverian troops turned and fled. The battle was over in ten minutes with a glorious victory for the clansmen.[29]

Off the field of battle, Charles was less successful in the Lowlands. The people were virtually unmoved by his pleas for assistance. The large numbers of Lowland volunteers which he had anticipated failed to appear. The Lowlanders were prospering under the economic policies of the Hanoverians and so desired no governmental change.[30] Furthermore, Presbyterians feared the Stuarts would attempt once more to change the religious settlement. The pastor of Edinburgh's St. Cuthbert's Church prayed, "Bless the King! Thou knowest *what* King I mean. . . . As for that young man who has come among us to seek an earthly crown, we beseech Thee to take him to Thyself and give him a crown of glory."[31]

But Charles and his lieutenants decided to push on with an invasion of England. Moving out of Edinburgh, his forces took Carlisle on the west coast and then marched on south to Preston, Manchester, and Derby. Among the English population there was fear of the kilted invaders, since it was rumored, among other things, that the Highlanders delighted in eating little children.[32] At Derby the Jacobite army was only 130 miles from London, and there was great fear in the capital as George II prepared to withdraw. But at Derby the clan chiefs informed

Charles that their homesick, superstitious men refused to advance any farther from the Highlands. Charles had expected a warm reception in England and throngs of volunteers for his victorious army, but the English were either cold or hostile.[33]

December 6, 1745, was the turning point of the conflict as the Highlanders began their retreat to Scotland. Following them was a numerically superior army under the command of King George's son William, Duke of Cumberland. During this retreat the clansmen destroyed an army at Falkirk under the command of General Hawley, but even after this victory they continued their movement northward. The Duke of Cumberland trailed the clans back to the Highlands, and the two armies finally clashed at Culloden Moor in April of 1746. Cumberland had 9000 men, while Charles had only 5000 hungry troops who were exhausted from an all-night march. Cumberland attacked during a sleet storm which was blowing in the faces of the clansmen. The Gaels fought for a time, but when the loss of great numbers and the flight of some units were observed, the entire surviving force turned and ran. The Duke, of course, pursued the fleeting clansmen and in a great bloodbath cut down the Highlanders in flight or hunted them out in the hills.[34] The savagery with which he put down the revolution earned for him the name of "Butcher Cumberland" in Scotland.   Little wonder that the flower named for him and called Sweet William in England is known as Stinking Billy in Scotland.[35]

Prince Charles did not die with his men in battle as he had promised, but fled from the field at Culloden. During the next five months, he roamed the Highlands and Islands garbed as a Highlander of low rank. Although there was a tempting price of £30,000 on his head, none of the Highlanders betrayed him. Part of the time he assumed the disguise of a serving maid to a plucky young Highland woman named Flora McDonald, who was later imprisoned for her role in his escape. In September of 1746, Charles finally embarked for France. With the departure of Prince Charles, the episode was closed.[36] Thereafter, the Highlanders' feelings of hatred, defiance, and remorse could be expressed only in their poems and songs. Hundreds of these Jacobite verses survive:

> The Stuarts ancient free-born race
> Now must we all give over;
> And we must take into their place
> The bastards of Hanover.[37]

In 1746 the British government began the enactment of a series of laws designed to destroy the clans and to bring the Highlands under political supervision. These restrictive laws applied to all clans alike, although most clans had not taken part in the rebellion and some had actually joined the Duke of Argyle and the Campbells in fighting for the House of Hanover.[38] By the Disarming Act of 1746, all weapons were taken from the Highlanders, who were forbidden to render military service to their chiefs.[39] At the same time, the Highland Dress Act deprived the clansman of "the cloaths commonly called *highland cloaths,* that is to say, the plaid, philebeg, or little kilt, trowse, shoulder-belts, or any part whatsoever of what peculiarly belongs to the highland garb."[40] With the passage of the bill taking from the clan chiefs all "heritable Jurisdictions," the area became subject to the laws of the realm. Justice was then administered by Sheriff-substitutes and local Justices of the Peace.[41] Finally, the estates of many of the chiefs of the Forty-five were confiscated.[42] As a result of these acts, the special bond between chief and clansman was effectively broken. The feudal, patriarchal Highland clan system came to an end as the chief became a landlord and the clansman a tenant or subtenant.

In addition, the London authorities instituted new religious policies aimed at Episcopalians and Catholics, in order to prevent other Jacobite revolutions. Presbyterians, Episcopalians, and Catholics all had been represented in the Jacobite army. The latter two groups had religious reasons for taking part, since each hoped for a religious settlement more favorable to its own church. The Highland Presbyterians who joined Charles did so for clan or for political reasons. We have already noted that the solidly Presbyterian Lowlands would not give support to Catholic Prince Charles in spite of his promises of religious freedom.[43]

The Presbyterian pastors of the Lowlands warned of the consequences flowing from a Stuart victory:

> Instead of a sleep in your pews,
> You'll be vex'd with repeating the creed;
> You'll be dunn'd and demurr'd with their news,
> If this their damn'd project succeed.
> Their mass and their set forms of prayer
> Will then in our pulpits take place:
> We must kneel till our breeches are bare,
> And stand at the glore and the grace.[44]

To this charge the Jacobites answered:

> To set our king upon the throne,
> Not church or state to overthrow,
> As wicked preachers falsely tell,
> The clans are coming, oho! oho!
> Therefore forbear, ye canting crew:
> Your bugbear tales are a' for show:

> The want of stipend is your fear,
> The clans are coming, oho! oho![45]

But the clans were soon fleeing, and when the fighting had ended, the government set forth new laws to arrest the influence of the Jacobite Episcopal and Catholic clergy. Non-juring pastors and priests were forbidden to preach, teach, or officiate at meetings. Both the leaders and any persons attending such illegal gatherings were threatened with imprisonment and "transportation."[46]

With the old religious, military, and clan leadership removed, the Jacobites of the Highlands were never again a threat to the peace of the British Isles.

CHAPTER II

THE EXILE THEORY

Farewell, farewell, dear Caledon,
Land of the Gael no longer!
A stranger fills thy ancient throne
In guile and treachery stronger.
Thy brave and just fall in the dust,
On ruin's brink they quiver;
Heaven's pitying e'e is clos'd on thee,
Adieu! adieu for ever!

—from *The Jacobite Relics.*[1]

IN THE THREE decades following the Forty-five, thousands of Highlanders flocked to America. More of them settled in North Carolina than in any other colony. What was responsible for this migration? American historians who have studied this movement believe the North Carolina Highlanders were forced into exile. These writers note that, although social and economic factors may have been involved, the major reason for the migration was political—the persecution and expatriation of rebel Highlanders after the Forty-five. This emphasis on the political origins of the migration appears with some variations in all histories that discuss the Highland settlement in North Carolina, and it is in need of careful examination.

The first historical work to deal with the upper Cape Fear settlement was *The History of North Carolina,* by

Francois-Xavier Martin, a refugee French printer who worked for a time in New Bern. Martin wrote in 1829 concerning the origins of the settlement:

In the latter part of the year 1746, the leaders of the adherents of the unfortunate prince Charles Edward, having perished on the scaffold, a general pardon passed the great seal, exempting from trial and punishment nineteen individuals out of twenty among the rest, on their being transported to America: they drew lots for this purpose. They were accompanied by a number of others, who, though they had not taken up arms, favored the prince's cause, and voluntarily shared the exile of their countrymen. A considerable number of them came to North Carolina, settled on Cape Fear river and formed the settlement in the middle of which the present town of Fayetteville now stands.[2]

Almost two decades later, in 1846, the Reverend William H. Foote published his *Sketches of North Carolina,* a history of the Presbyterian settlements within that state. In his capacity as Secretary of Foreign Missions, Foote visited most of the Presbyterian congregations in North Carolina. He conversed with clergymen and laymen, recorded significant pieces of information, and later compiled his materials in his history. Foote was greatly interested in the congregations of Highlanders and devoted a large part of *Sketches of North Carolina* to them. His book has been widely read and his interpretation of the origins of the colony—which agrees with Martin's account—has been widely accepted. Referring to the Highlanders imprisoned by the English, he wrote:

. . . a large number were pardoned, on condition of their emigrating to the plantations, after having taken the solemn oath of allegiance. *This is the origin of the large settlements of Highlanders on Cape Fear River* [Foote's italics]. For a large number who had taken arms for the Pretender preferred exile to death, or subjugation in their native land; and during the years 1746 and 1747, with their families and the families of many of their friends, removed to North Carolina and settled along the Cape Fear River, occupying a large space of country of which Crosscreek, afterwards Campbelton, now Fayetteville, was the centre. . . . This wilderness become [*sic*] a refuge to the harassed Highlanders; and shipload after shipload landed at Wilmington in 1746 and 1747. The emigration once fairly begun by royal authority and clemency was carried on by those who wished to improve their condition. . . .[3]

All later writers who have described the settlement of Highlanders in North Carolina have followed in varying degrees the tradition of Foote and Martin. The Reverend Eli Caruthers in his *Old North State* (1854) repeated the same account of the forced exile of Jacobites in North Carolina and quoted Foote as his source.[4] Another minister-historian, the Reverend Richard Webster, writing in 1857, also used Foote and explained the settlement in terms of the banishment of the Scottish rebels.[5] A third clergyman, the Reverend James G. Craighead, author of *Scotch and Irish Seeds in American Soil* (1878), acknowledged that some of the Highlander settlers were "voluntary exiles" but insisted that "most of them had fled from Scotland to avoid persecution and even death itself."[6]

Twentieth-century writers have followed the same vein. In 1900 the *Historical Account of the Settlements of Scotch Highlanders in America* was published by John P. MacLean. MacLean discussed at length the agricultural and social factors behind the migration, but he also added:

Left without chief, or protector, clanship broken up, homes destroyed and kindred murdered, dispirited, outlawed, insulted and without hope of palliation or redress, the only ray of light pointed across the Atlantic where peace and joy was to be found in the unbroken forests of North Carolina. Hence, during the years 1746 and 1747, great numbers of Highlanders, with their families and the families of their friends, removed to North Carolina and settled along the Cape Fear River, covering a great space of country, of which Cross Creek, or Campbellton, now Fayetteville, was the common center. This region received shipload after shipload of the harassed, down-trodden and maligned people. This emigration, forced by royal persecution and authority, was carried on by those who desired to improve their conditions, by owning the land they tilled.[7]

The next historian to discuss the settlement of Highlanders on the Cape Fear River was Charles A. Hanna. In Volume II of *The Scotch-Irish,* he devotes several sections to the topic. Again the explanation of the migration is almost word for word the same:

A large number [of prisoners] were pardoned on condition of their emigrating to the plantations, after having taken a solemn oath of allegiance. This was the origin of many of the Scottish settlements on the Cape Fear River; a considerable number of those who had taken up arms for the Pretender preferred exile to death, or to subjugation in their native land. During the years 1746 and 1747, these people, with their families, and many of their friends removed to North Carolina, occupying a large expanse of country along the Cape Fear, of which Campbelltown (now Fayetteville) was the centre. This wilderness became a refuge to the harassed Highlanders. Shipload after shipload landed at Wilmington in 1746 and 1747. The emigration once fairly begun by royal authority was carried on by those who wished to improve their condition. . . .[8]

Both Enoch W. Sikes, in Volume I of *The South in the Building of the Nation* (1909), and Herbert Osgood, in his *American Colonies of the Eighteenth Century* (1924), used Foote as their authority and repeated the description of a large emigration to America after Culloden.[9]

Robert D. W. Connor, formerly Secretary of the North Carolina Historical Commission, in Volume I of his masterly *History of North Carolina* (1919), presented a comprehensive picture of the many problems in the Highlands after 1746 and related these problems to the emigration movement. Dr. Connor clearly showed that the Highlanders were driven to North Carolina by poverty and agricultural displacement, but he also added that they came because "the king offered a pardon to all who would take the oath of allegiance and emigrate."[10]

The history of North Carolina by Samuel A'Court Ashe was published in 1925. In this work, too, the persecution after Culloden was treated as a direct cause of the colonization of the upper Cape Fear region. Ashe included interesting new detail about the transportation of entire clans when he wrote:

[A] pardon was issued under the great seal exempting from the death penalty nineteen out of twenty who had escaped the terrible slaughter. To determine who should be the victims of the melancholy fate, there was resort to the haphazard chance of casting the lot. Those undefended by fortune perished, the other nineteen being adjudged to suffer only expatriation. . . . The removal of entire clans was enforced and hundreds who, not being involved in the trouble, might have remained in their desolated country preferred to . . . share the fortunes of their compatriots rather than remain in their deserted homes. . . . in 1746 the vicinity of Fayetteville was occupied by a considerable colony of these unhappy Scotchmen, and shipload after shipload of these unfortunate people disembarked at Wilmington and then penetrated far into the wilderness of the interior.[11]

Since the appearance of Ashe's book, parts of the Martin-Foote thesis have appeared in *Some Eighteenth Century Tracts Concerning North Carolina,* edited by William K. Boyd;[12] *The Coming of the Scot,* by John H.

Finley of Princeton;[13] and *North Carolina: The History of a Southern State*, by Hugh T. Lefler and Albert R. Newsome.[14] Finally, Thomas J. Wertenbaker followed in the same tradition in his 1945 lecture at the University of Glasgow. In the paper, entitled "Early Scotch Contributions to the United States," Dr. Wertenbaker asserted: "[W]hen Prince Charles' men were hunted down by the Duke of Cumberland, some were permitted to choose exile as an alternative to the gallows. Of these a very large proportion came to North Carolina, landing at Wilmington and then moving west through the forests to settle in the vicinity of the present Fayetteville."[15]

The several works quoted above vary in some details but most, if not all, would agree with the three following propositions: (1) Many Highlanders came to North Carolina immediately after Culloden (the dates 1746 and 1747 appear frequently). (2) Of the Highlanders captured during the rebellion, nineteen out of twenty were pardoned on condition they would migrate to the colonies and many came to North Carolina. (One source speaks of whole clans' being expelled.) (3) The expatriated Highlanders were followed shortly by relatives, friends, and other Jacobite sympathizers. In the light of present available evidence, this historical tradition is without foundation. The Martin-Foote account of persecuted Highlanders' fleeing to North Carolina immediately after the Forty-five has been accepted by succeeding generations of historians. Contemporary American and British documents, however, contradict this traditional view.[16]

In eighteenth-century American documents and sources there appear no indications of a settlement of pardoned Highlanders on the Cape Fear immediately after the Forty-five. *The Colonial Records of North Carolina* contain no mention of such a settlement. The charges brought by the Palatine settlers in 1747—that they were being evicted from their lands in order to settle "the Rebels the Scots in our Possessions"—apparently were trumped up to gain sympathy from George II's Board of Trade.[17]   In his book, *Colonists in Bondage,* Abbot E. Smith describes the exile of Highland prisoners.   He gives evidence to show that these men landed in other colonies but not in North Carolina. Smith does point to the Palatine charges against Governor Johnson as an indication that some Highland Jacobites were in the colony,[18] but there are no colonial records to show that the Palatine settlers were replaced by Scottish rebels.   In this case, the land in question was on the Neuse, not the Cape Fear, River. There are no colonial documents describing a Highland settlement on the Neuse River.   Governor Gabriel Johnston, who was charged by others besides the Palatines with having sympathy for the Jacobites and with taking part in the alleged conspiracy to evict the Palatines in favor of the Highland rebels, wrote in 1749, "Tho I have made enquiry since this malicious report has reached me I can't Hear of One Person concerned in the late Rebellion, who has come into this Province."[19]   Johnston's political enemies composed long lists of petty charges in a determined effort to link him to the Jacobites.[20]   Had there been a settlement of pardoned Jacobites on the Neuse or Cape Fear rivers, certainly the Governor's critics would have specifically pointed to that settlement as proof of his Stuart sympathies.   Such a settlement was never mentioned.

British sources likewise fail to indicate that Jacobites were transported to North Carolina or that groups of Highlanders departed for America shortly after Culloden. The total number of Jacobite prisoners held by the British at the end of the rebellion has been computed at

3471. Of this number, 936 were ordered transported to
the colonies. Ninety-two per cent of the 936, or 866, were
sentenced to "Transportation with Indenture." Eight per
cent, or a total of seventy prisoners, were sentenced to
transportation without mention of terms of indenture. As
a result of death, unexpected pardon, or the act of turning
king's witness, 142 of the number appear to have escaped
their judgment, since there are records of only 794 prisoners transported to the colonies. These prisoners were
transported in eleven groups which left England between
March, 1747, and November, 1748.[21]

The terms of transportation originally specified that
the prisoners to be indentured were "to serve . . . in our
Colonies in America during the term of their natural
lives."[22] In practice, and later by decree, it was established that the indentures were only for seven-year terms;
but the prisoners were banished from the British Isles for
life.[23] There was no opportunity for this larger group to
take their families to the New World. They were put
aboard ship while still in irons and transported immediately.[24]

Indentured servants arriving in the colonies could not
have acted as free agents to establish a settlement because
they were sold as servants for a seven-year term, usually
to an established farmer. The ships of indentured prisoners were consigned to the West Indies and Maryland.[25]
It was official policy to notify the Governor when a ship-
ment of prisoners was sent to a colony.[26] The *Colonial
Records of North Carolina* fail to reveal any such notification.

The smaller group, which was transported without
being forced into indenture, included former officers.[27]
The *Scots Magazine* for May, 1748, was probably speaking of these prisoners when it reported that three pris-

oners were allowed to choose their place of banishment
and that one of them, a Mr. Farquharson, was granted
"leave to come to Scotland about his affairs before he
goes off."[28]   It is conceivable that the prisoners in this
group might have taken their families along to America
or had them follow, but there is no record either in
American or British sources of their having done so.

Immediately after the rebellion had been halted at the
battle of Culloden, there were proposals to transport
whole clans of Highlanders to America.   There was also
immediate opposition to the plan.[29]   Duncan Forbes,
President of the Court of Session in Scotland, entertained
the plan of transporting "the most active and dangerous"
of the Highland groups to America.[30]   The Privy Council
considered the proposal by the Duke of Cumberland that
certain of the disaffected clans, such as the Camerons and
the McDonalds, be transported.   It evidently was not
considered feasible since the plan did not emerge from
the Privy Council.[31]   The Parliament that same year
passed bills to disarm the Highlanders, to deprive them
of their distinctive dress, and to enforce the law among
them; but the proposal to transport clans did not receive
Parliamentary consideration and was not alluded to in
the debates on the above bills.[32]   The *Gentlemen's Magazine,* the *London Magazine,* and the *Scots Magazine* reported the transportation of prisoners but did not mention either the expulsion of clans or the voluntary departure of Highlanders.   Bishop Robert Forbes, the
scrupulous Jacobite historian, designed his work, *The Lyon
in Mourning,* to document the events of the Forty-five
and the treatment of the Highlanders after Culloden.[33]
His three volumes are collections of manuscripts by eye-
witnesses.   They often refer to the "Cruelties after Culloden" but fail to mention the transportation of either

prisoners or clans to North Carolina, or any immediate emigration of rebels.

Finally, an examination of American documents dealing with the North Carolina land grants is revealing.[34] The rate of land-grant issuance is not a perfect guide to immigration rates since some immigrants did not secure land grants and since Scotch-Irish names cannot easily be separated from the names of Highlanders. There does, however, appear to be a relationship between the Highlander immigration rate and the number of land grants made in North Carolina to what appear to be Highlanders. We know that in 1739 a group of 350 people from Argyllshire settled in North Carolina.[35] Land grant statistics for the year 1740 reflect their arrival, and this is some corroboration of the reliability of these statistics.

From 1738 to 1751, the following numbers of land grants were issued to people with Highland names in the Cape Fear counties of New Hanover and Bladen:

Year	Number of grants	Year	Number of grants
1738:	0	1745:	5
1739:	0	1746:	5
1740:	33	1747:	0
1741:	3	1748:	2
1742:	1	1749:	6
1743:	0	1750:	2
1744:	0	1751:	2

The rebellion which began in 1745 was not terminated until the spring of 1746. Had there been a sizable influx of Highlander settlers into North Carolina in the years 1746 and 1747, the land grant figures should register the increase. Indentured servants, of course, would not have received land grants, but many of those prisoners transported without indenture and those who "voluntarily shared the exile of their countrymen" would have. It was crown policy to issue land grants to anyone capable of tilling the land, on payment of only a small fee to cover surveying and registration costs. Quitrents were not collected for two years after grant issuance. It will be explained more fully in chapter v that the average Highland tenant, upon sale of his livestock and tools, was able to pay transportation costs to America and land-grant fees. Sometimes, as appears to be the case in the 1739 migration, the tacksmen who led the migration paid all transportation costs, and those who made the voyage agreed to work for the tacksmen for a specified time. When that occurred, many land grants were issued to the migration leaders. However, the statistics for 1746-51 show that no such large numbers of grants were made. It should be noted that, of the 1746 total of five land grants to people with Scottish Highlander names, three of the individuals had received land grants before 1745 and were not new settlers.[36] Of the 1749 total of six, two had received grants before 1745.[37] Thus, the rate of land-grant issuance to Highlanders during the years 1746-51 was at a relatively stable and low level. There is no evidence here to indicate a migration of any size into the upper Cape Fear area in that period.

In summary, that the North Carolina settlement of Highlanders on the upper Cape Fear was enlarged by the coming of numbers of pardoned Jacobites in 1746 and 1747 is an interpretation that is, on the basis of present evidence, subject to grave doubt. The large group of pardoned rebels who were transported to America came as indentured servants, not as settlers. A smaller group transported to the colonies conceivably might have established a settlement, but there are neither American nor British sources to substantiate the point. Although the expulsion of disloyal clans was suggested to the Privy Council, it was not attempted. A survey of land grants to people with Highland names who lived in the Cape Fear counties does not reveal an increase immediately after the rebellion of 1745. Finally, it should be remembered that Governor Gabriel Johnston denied in 1749 that any Jacobites lived in the colony. The defeat of the Highlanders in the Forty-five may be classified only as an indirect factor in the migration to North Carolina. The defeat produced far-reaching social and economic changes which, in turn, caused some Highlanders to leave their native land. But there is nothing to indicate that pressure from the British government forced the Highlanders to flee to North Carolina after the Forty-five.

CHAPTER III

MOTIVES FOR MIGRATION

The glen that was my father's own
Must be by his forsaken;
The house that was my father's home
Is levell'd with the brucken.
Ochon! ochon! our glory's o'er,
Stole by a mean deceiver!
—from *The Jacobite Relics.*[1]

IN CONTRAST to the previously noted explanations of the migration of Highlanders to the New World, eighteenth-century British observations pointed primarily to nonpolitical reasons. They stated that the Highlanders were flocking to America because of these interrelated factors: (1) The changes in agriculture produced rack rents and evictions. (2) The decay of the clan system removed the social ties and restraints that might have prevented migration. (3) The growth of population contributed to poverty and unrest. I will examine these factors consecutively.

The revolution of 1745 was followed by a transformation of agriculture in the Highlands. This in turn produced far-reaching changes in the lives of the inhabitants of the area. Earlier agricultural improvements in the Lowlands had not spread northward beyond the mountain barriers, largely because of the political and social conditions in the North. However, after 1746, innovations in agriculture were slowly introduced. There were a number of reasons for the new developments. The Turnpike Road Act of 1751 provided roads for ready access to the area.[2] Men who had formerly spent their days in the retinue of a chieftain were now freed from such responsibility. Without clan ties, the Highland population became far more mobile. The chiefs who earlier had been concerned with "man-rent" (i.e., warrior service) now began to exploit their lands for the largest possible return of money rent. The results of these changes were three: the old system of land leasing was revised, new crops and farming methods were adopted, and numbers of unneeded tenants were forced from their holdings.

The change in land holding centered about the abolition of the tacksman (middleman) who formerly had exercised an important function in the tribal society. Since the power of a chief depended upon the number of clansmen responding to his call, a reliable system of muster had been developed. The system involved the chief's granting of leases, or tacks, to near relatives, giving them control of parcels of land in return for token rents and the promise of military service. The tacksman, or lease holder, then divided the greater part of the land into smaller plots, "subsetting" it to groups of tenants, who farmed it in common and who agreed to give military service. Beneath the tenants were the cotters, or subtenants, who formed still another group. These were employed as laborers by the tenants and tacksmen. The tacksmen were primarily the organizers or lieutenants of the military group.[3]

Although the military need for tacksmen was absent after 1746, these middlemen continued to function in the process of land leasing. As a group, they were wealthy.

Tacksmen held long leases from the lairds calling for nominal rents. While the tacksman paid a small rent and held a long lease, the tenant usually received a short lease and his rent became so high that he lived in constant fear of bad crops. He was, in addition, liable for the payment of "grassums," or special fees, on the frequent renewals of the lease.[4] Johnson records the Highland characterization of the tacksman as "a drone . . . living upon the product of an estate without the right of property, or the merit of labour, and who impoverishes at once the landlord and the tenant."[5] Since a tacksman's obligation to his chief had been figured largely in military terms, an upward revision of the rents was inevitable when military service became obsolete. Whenever a tacksman's lease expired, the laird assured himself a greater income by substantially increasing the rent upon renewal or by auctioning the lease. The latter act injured the tacksman, since tacks long had been considered hereditary.[6] Pennant noted that though the buyer frequently was unable to pay the inflated rent agreed upon, the price of a tack was often doubled by auction.[7] An America-bound tacksman from Inverness-shire voiced a common complaint in 1773 that his rent had risen fourfold from £5 to £20 in the twenty years prior to his emigration.[8]

The tacksmen, of course, attempted to pass the rent rise on to their tenants, and in most cases the attempt was made before the introduction of improved agricultural methods or household industries. Hence, in Pennant's observations, "the great men begin at the wrong end, . . . squeezing the bag, before they have helped the poor tenant to fill it."[9] But the tacksmen were largely unsuccessful in raising their tenants' rents for the reason that tenants were already paying to the limit of their capacity. The record book of William Mackintosh, a tacksman in Inverness-shire, shows that between the years 1769 and 1780 he normally could collect only half of his rents and that in bad seasons he received less than a third.[10] When the tacksman could not successfully pass on the rent rise, he was forced to pay the increment from his own resources. When he was no longer able to pay the rents, he cast his eyes westward and made plans to emigrate. James Boswell visited the celebrated Flora McDonald in the early 1770's, and he found her voicing the same complaint. "She talked as if her husband and family would emigrate, rather than be oppressed by their landlord."[11] The McDonalds departed for North Carolina in 1774.

Another phase of agricultural change was the introduction of new methods of production. Formerly, land had been tilled by the "run-rig" system. Under this system, a group of tenants rented the land in common from a tacksman. Lots were drawn to decide which strip or ridge each tenant would till. Plowing was done cooperatively and, in some places, cultivation and harvesting, too.[12] With such a farming system there was no incentive for liming, draining, or otherwise improving fields, since a tenant could never be certain he would work the same ridges again. The absence of enclosures meant that selective breeding was impossible and that crops were constantly in danger of destruction from wandering cattle. Neither crop rotation nor field rotation was practiced. The "infields" near the farmyard received some manure and were constantly under oats and barley. The "outfields," which consisted of less fertile land and which received little manure, were tilled until they were exhausted. They then were allowed to lie fallow until strengthened.[13]

Enlightened lairds were aware that this type of farming would never allow the tenants a return adequate for an improved standard of living or for the payment of higher rents, and they therefore suggested new farming methods.[14]   Other lairds, motivated only by self-interest, simply raised the rents whenever possible.[15]   The *Edinburgh Advertiser* was particularly concerned about this latter group when it published the following advice on the proper way to increase rents:

It is in vain to tell a poor ignorant prejudiced tenant, two hundred miles from all civility and refinement, that he shall pay double or treble his former rent; this is oppression. First give them the power of doing it; set them examples of what good husbandry is; take farmers, and implements from England; let the poor people see the effects of industry and improvement; inclose their lands; give them grass feeds, and take every measure for introducing plenty of green winter food of the hardier kinds for their cattle, that the meal appropriated to feed their children may not in hard times be taken for their cows. Let them see the contrast of their own misery, and the happiness of a different system. Let this work some effect in making them industrious and willing before you think of raising. Let the rise be disguised; perform necessary works for them which you know will pay greatly, and take the return in rent; at the moment they pay a rise, then they will feel the fairness, and even the benefit of it . . . but to act on different, on the old principles, is only to court disappointment for yourself, and to send the people to America.[16]

But these techniques were largely ignored as rents went up regardless of conditions. The rise in rents tended to drive out numbers of both the tacksmen and tenant groups. Lairds were not grieved by the tacksmen's departure since they might now receive the full economic value of the land without sharing it with the tacksmen. New leases were granted directly to the former tenants of the tacksmen. The new leases specified that the land

was not to be sublet and thus prevented the new lease-
holders from becoming tacksmen. At the same time,
the services owed by tenants to tacksmen (e.g., aid up to
forty days a year in plowing, cutting turf, spreading
manure, and cutting peats) were abolished.[17] Tenants
could spend this time improving their own plots. The
effect of these changes was to remove the tacksmen as a
privileged class. Tacksmen who did not emigrate were
lowered in social status, while the tenants who now were
the recipients of longer leases were raised in status. Farming was placed on a business basis, as clan relationships
were forgotten.[18]

Slowly but steadily during the last half of the eighteenth century, agricultural methods changed. "Run-
rigs" were replaced by compact, enclosed farms which
encouraged tenants to improve the holding and which
allowed selective breeding. The "outfield" and "in-
field" system was discarded for a system of field and
crop rotation. Large areas of swamp, heretofore considered untillable, became valuable farm land after being drained. When the English iron plow was tried in
the Highlands, it proved far superior to the old wooden
harrow. Turnips, rutabagas, peas, and kale were adopted
as rotation crops and as new foods. Flax, which the
government introduced in hope of starting a linen industry, did not grow well; but potatoes thrived and within two decades were the staple food in some areas. To
fertilize the thin soil, limestone, which was plentiful in
many sections, was burned in peat fires and spread upon
the land. These new techniques and crops transformed
agricultural life in the Highlands.[19] It must be pointed
out, however, that the adoption of new farming methods
was not always uniform throughout the Highlands. As
late as 1814, tacksmen were still found in several areas;

and in others the "run-rig" system persisted at the end of the eighteenth century.[20]

Equally far-reaching changes occurred in grazing, which was the most important agricultural activity of the Highlands. Both before and after the Forty-five, black cattle constituted the major export from the region. Each fall, cattle drivers bought animals at several Highland markets, divided them into herds of one to two thousand, and drove them south for sale in the Lowlands and in England. Isabel F. Grant estimated that in the latter part of the eighteenth century 100,000 cattle annually were exported.[21]

Scarcity of fodder in winter was the great problem for cattle raisers. Few farmers had sufficient hay.[22] A contemporary estimated mortality among cattle each winter at one in five.[23] Flora McDonald wrote that her husband Allan lost 327 head of cattle in the three winters before they came to America.[24] The weakness of cattle during the winter because of insufficient food was aggravated by the Highland custom of bleeding cattle for food. When Captain Edward Burt was in the Highlands, he found that by spring cattle were frequently too weak to stand. The animals were so feeble, in fact, that they often had to be lifted to their feet in the morning and sometimes carried to pasture.[25]

Although cattle continued as the main export, Lowland sheep were brought into the Highlands after the Forty-five. Since the sheep graziers could afford to pay rents considerably higher than the farmers, sheep farming was encouraged by the lairds.[26] Sheep herding began in Perthshire in the 1760's, and only a decade later the practice had spread to the northernmost part of the Highlands. With the sheep came enclosures and displaced tenants. The *Scots Magazine* in 1772 lamented the large number of Sutherland tenants forced to move to North Carolina because their farms were turned into pastures.[27] Three years later the *Scots Magazine* noted the expulsion of large numbers of tenants in Perth and Argyllshire for the same reason.[28] One displaced and indignant Highlander cried out:

> When the bold kindred, in the time long-vanish'd,
> Conquer'd the soil and fortified the keep,
> No seer foretold the children would be banish'd,
> That a degenerate lord might boast his sheep.[29]

In 1773, the British government, alarmed by reports of a large movement to America, ordered port inspectors to compose lists of emigrants leaving British ports. Records have been preserved for the period January 1, 1774, through September, 1775. Since many persons left from small ports that did not have inspectors, the reports are not complete. Some records give names, ages, and occupations of emigrants as well as their particular reasons for leaving; others list only the number aboard ship and generalize about the reasons for their departure. These records agree that rack rent was the major factor in the emigration. North Carolina is listed as the destination of 468 Highlanders. Of this group, sixty-nine family heads clearly identified themselves as farmers, and all but four stated that they were leaving their native land because of high rents.[30]

According to a Highland correspondent for the *Scots Magazine* in 1773, "the extravagant rents extracted by the landlords is the sole cause given for this spirit of emigration."[31] In the same journal a year earlier, a lengthy article agreed that rents were the key to the emigration and suggested the establishment of an impartial panel of judges to set the rents.[32] In two other instances, the *Scots*

Magazine affirmed that high rents were the major cause of the exodus.[33]   Thomas Pennant grieved that this economic pressure forced many to exchange their native land for what he called the "wilds of America."[34]   Bishop Forbes, the meticulous historian of the Forty-five and its aftermath, summed up the majority opinion of eighteenth-century observers when he wrote despairingly in 1771, "All, *all*, this is owing to the exorbitant rents for land."[35]

There is evidence of agricultural factors other than high rents contributing to the migration—factors which varied from north to south in the Highlands.   In the northern counties of Sutherland and Caithness, there occurs but a single report of tenants' being turned out because of sheep enclosures.[36]   The more characteristic complaint of the northern tenant in the 1770's was that "the Rent . . . was raised to double at the same time that the price of cattle was reduced one half."[37]   Some cotters lost their employment when new farming implements and methods were adopted.   At the same time, some tenants who formerly cultivated small "run-rig" plots and grazed cattle in the large common pasture found that they could not make an adequate income on a small enclosed plot where only limited grazing was possible.[38]   Other complaints related to the failure of crops because of early frosts, the loss of cattle in the spring, and the exaction of services up to thirty or forty days a year.[39]   In the South there is little mention of services, but more references to poverty as a reason for emigration.[40]   Thomas Pennant found that as early as 1750 poverty caused such a "depression of spirit" among the inhabitants of the island of Skye that groups of them were sailing for America.[41]   In the southern Highlands, the greatest cry was against the shepherds.   Emigrants from Appin in Argyllshire estimated in 1775 that one-third of the land in their area had been converted to sheep pasture.[42] The Lowland shepherds who moved into the Highlands found that, when they grazed their sheep under equal conditions with Highland cattle, they could produce three pounds of mutton for each pound of beef. Besides this, they received income from the sale of wool. Since shepherds could easily pay double the former rents, lairds in Argyllshire and Perthshire had pecuniary incentives to evict their tenants and enclose the land for flocks.[43]

The manuscripts of James Hogg, a tacksman from Caithness who came to North Carolina in 1774 with 280 Highlanders, are the most valuable extant American sources for the study of the Highland emigration. Hogg described in colorful language and in detail the particular problems of his agricultural area, the method of recruitment used by him, and the voyage to America. Unlike most tacksmen, he praised his laird. He cited the absence of law and order as the reason for his departure. Although Hogg was the only known emigrant to make this charge, his complaints are sufficiently explicit to merit examination. Hogg's turnips, carrots, potatoes, and peas were stolen from his fields before harvest time.[44] A man who purloined a sheep from him was found guilty and was banished but returned immediately to Caithness "protected and sheltered by a gentleman of his name."[45] When a band of ruffians set fire to Hogg's house and attacked his family in 1772, he was able to obtain a conviction only after lengthy and expensive efforts.[46] Hence, when his brother from North Carolina visited Caithness and invited him to move to the New World, Hogg was, in his words,

. . . easily determined to leave a country, where, for want of police, and due administration of the laws, I had found it impossible to defend my goods from being stolen; . . . and life was daily exposed to the resentment of murderous ruffians; and where the thief, the robber, the murderer, and willful fire-raiser, never hitherto wanted a gentleman, or rather a party of gentlemen to patronize them.[47]

There are conflicting reports about the honesty and respect for law of the Highlanders after the Forty-five. Samuel Johnson found their former inclination to thievery "very much represt."[48]   Few doors were equipped with fastenings in spite of the general poverty of the people.[49]   On the other hand, Captains John Beckwith and Walter Johnston, English officers of occupation in the Highlands, referred to the people as "notorious thieves" and "notorious plunderers." They complained that the criminals of the Highlands "have always been protected by men of estate."[50]

The main obstacle to justice was probably the sense of clan brotherhood which persisted in some areas. This tie caused men of one name to thwart justice to save a guilty brother. Since the men who set fire to James Hogg's house were of the same clan as the sheriff, the sheriff connived with the arsonists against Hogg. Clan loyalty— supporting a kinsman, right or wrong—was bound to interfere with the workings of justice. A famous incident which shows how clansmen could use the law to their advantage resulted from the murder of Colin Campbell in 1752. Two Stewarts, Alan Breck and James of the Glen, were charged with the crime. Alan escaped to France but James was seized and tried. Robert Louis Stevenson used the incident as part of the plot in *Kidnapped*. In the book Alan Breck Stewart explains to his friend David his chance for justice when he says, "This is a Campbell that's been killed. Well, it'll be tried in Inverara, the Campbell's head place; with fifteen Campbells in the jury-box, and the biggest Campbell of all (and that's the Duke) sitting cocking the bench. Justice, David?"[51] In the actual trial, which did have a Campbell jury, James of the Glen was found guilty on doubtful evidence and hanged.[52]

It should be remembered that the transformation of Highland agriculture in the last half of the eighteenth century was possible only because the clan system with its social and military manifestations was decaying. Some of the clan ties persisted, as James Hogg discovered, but the intricate political, social, and economic system of old no longer functioned by the 1770's. This was a social change of major proportions.

Another motive for migration was the decay of the clan system. Before 1745 the chief was the unquestioned ruler of his clan. His word was law and absolute discipline was demanded. Life or death, war or peace, awaited his command. The clansman rejoiced to share his name, religion, and his dangers.[53] In this society, where exploitation might have been expected, power was tempered with benevolence. The chief's table was open to all and his counsel freely offered to the most humble.[54] Thus, in a society of marked distinctions, an intimacy developed which can best be expressed in family terms. Bound together by common devotion to a chief, the clan was an integrated family which prospered and suffered together, worked and warred together, lived and died together.

Parliament acted swiftly after the defeat of 1746 to cut the military and judicial ties between chief and clansmen. When the chiefs demanded economic returns to replace the former military dues, the problem of rents emerged. Many chiefs moved to the Lowlands or to England and sent factors to force the enclosure movement and administer the rise in rents.[55] By the 1770's, the bonds of kinship, devotion, and service, which had been the sinews of the tribal society, had been largely severed. "Scotus Americanus" charged the lairds with "luxury, dissipation and extravagance" and lamented that they were quite "unlike their fore-fathers."[56]   Samuel Johnson found a member of the clan Maclean at Iona in 1773 who still had such reverence for his chief that he exclaimed, "I would cut my bones for him; and if he had sent his dog for it, he should have had it."[57]   Still Johnson wrote that in the 1770's most clansmen had lost their respect for and sense of responsibility to the chiefs.[58]

While it is true that the clan structure was destroyed after 1746, signs of decay within the society could be seen earlier. A study of the lists of prisoners in the Forty-five shows that 200 out of 2590 clansmen named were unwilling to follow their chief into war and had to be "forced out" or "pressed."[59]   On the way south between Edinburgh and the English border, a thousand men deserted the Highland army.[60]   On another occasion a whole clan of McDonalds deserted.[61]   This decay or loosening of the tribal bands was more than a refusal of allegiance on the part of the clansmen; there is an example in 1739 of a betrayal of clansmen by their chiefs. MacLeod of Harris and MacDonald of Sleat in that year hired a press gang and ship to transport to America 110 clansmen whom they no longer desired as dependents. When the ship stopped in north Ireland they escaped. However, the great scandal this act created in the Highlands shows that it was an unusual occurrence.[62]

The chain of circumstances that caused the lairds to raise the rent, insist upon enclosure of land, and introduce sheep, all made the clansman feel that the chief had ceased to be his patron. No longer would the laird protect him in danger, feed him in want, or hear him in court. Janet Schaw, an America-bound Lowlander, was grieved at the sight of the Highland emigrants aboard her ship and amazed that their laird had treated them so callously. She described him as the "Hard-hearted, little Tyrant of yonder rough domains."[63]

Reports of America must have been received with considerable interest by unhappy Highlanders. The thirty-two-page pamphlet by the writer from Islay who assumed the nom de plume "Scotus Americanus" gives an idea of the information available to the discontented. The work, which is entitled *Informations Concerning the Province of North Carolina,* begins with an attack on the lairds, comparing them to Peter the Great and Louis XIV and then suggesting that "the Highlanders should seek for refuge in some happier land, on some more hospitable shore, where freedom reigns, and where, unmolested by Egyptian task-masters, they may reap the produce of their own labour and industry."[64] To Highlanders cursed with small patches of worn-out soil, "Scotus Americanus" spoke of the large, rich plots easily available across the Atlantic in a "wholesome" climate where "poverty is almost an entire stranger."[65]

Unfortunately we do not know how widely this tract was circulated, but we do know that America was thought of in idyllic terms. Even such an opponent of emigration as "Philopatriae," writing in the *Scots Magazine,* calls America the place of "life in abundance."[66] One emigrant, William Sutherland, said he was moving to Carolina because of "the assurances of the fertility of the land, which yields three crops a year."[67]

Quite apart from the printed pamphlets, and probably more influential, were the letters sent back to Scotland by the new settlers in America. On the ship *Bachelor of Leith,* which sailed from Caithness in 1774, over half indicated that they made their decision to migrate because of the encouraging accounts received from countrymen or relatives who had gone before them.[68]

Pamphlets and letters were not, in themselves, the basic reasons for the large Highland emigration of the eighteenth century. Why were a people noted for clannishness and provincialism willing to be transported to a new continent? New modes of land holding, cultivation, and grazing had produced high rents, enclosures, and evictions. Highlanders no longer protected or regulated by chief and clan organizations sought relief for economic woes in the New World.

> O where shall I gae seek my bread?
> Or where shall I gae wander?
> O where shall I gae hide my head?
> For here I'll bide nae langer.
> The seas may row, the winds may blow,
> And swathe me round in danger;
> My native land I must forego
> And roam a lonely stranger.[69]

The third major motive for migration was population pressure. Although the population rise in the Highlands of Scotland was not so sharp as in England in the eighteenth century, it was large enough to make more difficult the social and agricultural adjustments after the Forty-five.[70] Even in the first quarter of the century, there seemed to be more people than the economic resources of the area could support. In his preface to *Rob Roy*, Sir Walter Scott discussed the excess of population in the Highlands during the first years of the eighteenth century. To illustrate the point he repeated the words of Graham of Gartmore: "The people are extremely prolific, and therefore so numerous, that there is not business in that country, according to its present order and economy, for the one-half of them. Every place is full of idle people. . . ."[71] This situation became more critical when the number of inhabitants further increased in the last half of the century. In a rapidly expanding economy, this growing population might have been welcomed; in the Highland economy, even with the agricultural improvements after 1746, the increasing numbers were a constant problem.[72]

Why did the Highland population increase during the last half of the eighteenth century? There were many factors responsible. The new Highland roads, which were built originally to provide ready access for English troops, also served as commercial thoroughfares.[73] The failure of a crop in one section because of drought or frost could now be remedied with food products transported from more distant areas. The Forfeited Estates Board, which administered lands confiscated from rebel leaders after the Forty-five, had a surplus in its treasury which was used to buy food for afflicted areas.[74] Starvation and suffering were alleviated through this system.

There was also a medical reason for the population growth. It was during the 1760's and 1770's that vaccination for smallpox was begun in the Highlands.[75] Smallpox had long been a scourge. The cost of vaccination was substantial—two shillings and six pence per person—but in spite of the cost the landlord of the island of Muck in the Hebrides paid in 1774 for the vaccination of eighty people living on the island.[76] Pennant reported the vaccination process in Caithness and the Orkneys as highly successful in producing immunity.[77]

In addition to the alleviation of famine and the curbing of smallpox, the introduction of new crops (particularly potatoes and kale, which were more dependable and more productive than the old Highland oats) served to encourage a population rise. The potato, imported from

Ireland in 1743, was soon cultivated throughout the Highlands.[78]   Kale also became popular.   In the month of August, Johnson found the latter vegetable served at each meal.[79]   However, although potatoes and kale provided a higher subsistence level, which probably lowered the death rate, the cultivation of these foods did not provide many new jobs for the enlarged population.[80]

The remarkable fecundity of Highland couples was also related to the population rise.   The Lowland economist Adam Smith noted that even "a half-starved Highland woman frequently bears more than twenty children."[81]   This was possible since girls usually married in their early teens.   In the opinion of Burt, Highland parents displayed amazing indifference toward the welfare of their many offspring.   He observed:

The young Children of the ordinary Highlanders are miserable Objects indeed, and are mostly over-run with that Distemper which some of the old Men are hardly ever freed of from their Infancy.   I have often seen them come out from the Huts early in a cold Morning stark naked, and squat themselves down . . . like Dogs on a Dunghill. . . .   And at other Times they have but little to defend them from the Inclemencies of the Weather in so cold a Climate: nor are the Children of some Gentlemen in much better Condition, being strangely neglected till they are six or seven years old. . . .[82]

But in spite of such treatment, sufficient numbers of the children survived to push Highland population statistics ever upward.

Fortunately, reliable statistical sources exist to show the degree to which population increased in the second half of the eighteenth century.   The earliest systematic census of Scotland was taken in the year 1755 by the Reverend Alexander Webster of Edinburgh.   Webster, who was Moderator of the General Assembly of the

Church of Scotland, persuaded the Society for the Propagation of Christian Knowledge in the Highlands and
Islands to help him in his project. The Society ordered all
ministers in Presbyteries where the Society had Charity
Schools to count the inhabitants in their parishes. The
ministers were warned that failure to make the census
would result in withdrawal of the schools by the Society.
By these means, Webster was able to secure reports from
all the Highland and Island districts. In those Lowland
areas where the Society maintained few schools, Webster
sent his requests to the parish ministers and his position
as titular head of the church secured their co-operation.
Since Webster used the parish ministers as his census
takers, the reports were made by literate individuals with
previous experience in keeping church records.[83]

In the last years of the eighteenth century, another
census of Scotland was made by Sir John Sinclair. Census
forms were sent in 1790 to all ministers of the Church of
Scotland requesting information not only on population
but also on such subjects as housing, agricultural methods,
animal husbandry, roads, church affairs, and curiosities.
One hundred and sixty questions were asked in each
census form. Shortly thereafter, model reports from four
parishes were published and sent with a letter to all
ministers in Scotland urging the completion of their reports in a similar manner. In response to these requests,
413 (approximately half of the Scottish parish ministers)
submitted reports within a year. To obtain the co-operation of the rest, Sinclair then secured a resolution from the
General Assembly of the church asking all ministers to aid
the project. Leaders of the church and influential laymen
were enlisted to write personal letters to the recalcitrants
requesting their help. By these means Sinclair was able to
obtain reports from all but twenty-five parishes. To finish

the census, agents were sent to these twenty-five parishes. The work was complete by 1798 and was published in twenty volumes.[84]

By a comparison of Webster's census of 1755 with Sinclair's census of 1790-98, the population growth of the Highlands in the last half of the century can be obtained. Figure I records the population figures for each Highland shire or parish.[85]   In 1755, Webster computed the population of all of Scotland at 1,265,380; Sinclair's reports show that the population during the years 1790-98 was 1,526,-492.   According to these two authorities, during this forty-year period the population of all of Scotland increased by 261,112, while that of the Highland districts alone rose 37,527.[86]   Expressed in percentages, the population of Scotland expanded twenty-one per cent over its 1755 level in the forty years following Webster's census, but in the same time the number of Highland inhabitants rose only fourteen per cent over the 1755 level.

The population increase of 37,527 registered in Figure I is incomplete, since no account is taken of the large numbers of Highlanders who migrated either to the Lowlands or to America.   All subsequent Scottish census reports have dealt with the numbers migrating, but Webster and Sinclair made only short references to the emigration of the period and provided no statistics on its size.   If the number of those who left the Highlands were added to the 37,527 population rise recorded, the percentage of increase would be considerably larger than the fourteen per cent noted above and probably would be near the twenty-one per cent for all of Scotland.

Two contemporary estimates of the numbers moving to America vary considerably and refer to different years, but they provide some idea of the size of the migration. John Knox in 1784 stated that 20,000 Highlanders left for

FIGURE I. HIGHLAND POPULATION GROWTH, 1755-1798

	Webster 1755	Sinclair 1790-1798	Increase (%)	Decrease (%)
1. Argyllshire including Bute and Arran......	70,157	86,664	16,507 (23.5)	
2. Banff Kirkmichael.....	1288	1276		12 (.9)
3. Caithness..........	22,215	24,802	2587 (11.6)	
4. Cromarty..........	5163	5284	121 (2.3)	
5. Dumbarton Luss...........	978	917		61 (6.2)
Arroquhar......	466	379		87 (18.6)
6. Elgin Duthel.........	1785	1110		675 (37.8)
7. Inverness including all the Hebrides but Lewis..........	64,656	73,979	9323 (14.4)	
8. Nairn Nairn..........	1698	2400	702 (41.3)	
Ardclach........	1163	1186	23 (1.9)	
Calder..........	882	1062	180 (20.4)	
9. Perth Balquhidder.....	1592	1300		292 (18.3)
Blair...........	3257	3120		137 (4.2)
Callander......	1750	2100	350 (20.0)	
Comrie.........	2546	3000	454 (17.8)	
Dull...........	5748	4676		1072 (18.6)
Fortingall......	3859	3914	55 (1.4)	
Kenmore.......	3067	3463	396 (12.9)	
Killin..........	1968	2360	392 (19.9)	
Kirkmichael.....	2689	2200		489 (18.1)
Mouline........	2109	1749		287 (11.5)
Weem..........	1295	1364	69 (5.3)	360 (17.0)
10. Ross including the isle of Lewis........	42,493	50,146	7653 (18.0)	
11. Sutherland........	20,774	22,961	2187 (10.5)	
Total........	266,085	303,612 266,085	40,999 3,472	
		37,527	37,527	

America between 1763 and 1773. Another visitor in the Highlands, Thomas Garnett, estimated in 1800 that 30,000 had emigrated to America in the years 1773-75.[87] It must not be forgotten that, at the same time, many Highlanders were moving south to find work in the Lowlands. The Earl of Selkirk, who promoted a settlement of Highlanders in Nova Scotia, has described the rising population in and emigration from the island of Skye:

A gentleman of ability and observation, whose employment in the island gave him the best opportunities of information, estimates the total number who emigrated, between 1772 and 1791, at 4000. [As for] the number who, during the same period, went to the Low Country of Scotland . . . he considers 8000 as the least at which they can possibly be reckoned. Notwithstanding this drain, it appears that the natural tendency of population to increase has more than filled up the blank; and if, to the numbers which have left the island, we add the increase which has probably taken place among them also, in their new situation, we cannot doubt that there are now living a number of people descended from those who inhabited the island at the period of Dr. Webster's enumeration, at least, double of its actual population.[88]

It is not possible to state specifically the number of Highlanders who moved to the Lowlands and America, since there were no reliable contemporary surveys of the movement. It can be observed, however, that the movement to America must have been a large one because the Scottish periodicals of the day constantly report the departure of emigrant parties from all sections of the Highlands.[89] The movement to the Lowlands was discussed much less frequently and probably did not involve so large a group of people as the American migration.[90] In view of this double migration and the apparent great size of the latter, it is not improbable that the increase of population in the Highlands may well have been double the 37,527 that appears in Figure I.

What effect did the constantly increasing number of inhabitants have on agriculture? Arthur Young, the English agricultural expert, was concerned with this Highland problem. He was of the opinion that, though tenants would be reluctant to leave a considerate landlord, the growth of population would nevertheless produce unemployment and displacement. About the impact of the Seven Years War on the Highland population, he wrote, "It has been observed, that the war carried off between 50 and 60,000 of the ablest men in the north and west of Scotland, which, for a time, distressed every branch of demand, yet in a very few years the numbers were greater than ever, and hands for every demand so plentiful, that many wanted work. . . ."[91] In fact, this rise in population only aggravated the agricultural problems of the period. Enclosures, whether made for sheep farming or for general farming, resulted in the displacement of some of the families on the heavily populated estates.[92] Some sympathetic landlords were slow to evict the large families, of course, but it was the judgment of several contemporaries that, if all Highland farm land had been enclosed into adequate family-sized farms, there would have been room for only half the people in the Highlands.[93] This overpopulation led to fierce competition for the land leases offered at auction, and the resultant high rents made life even more precarious for the Highland farmer. The new farming methods had increased the productivity of agriculture—sometimes as much as tenfold—which meant fewer people starved, but the new farming methods did not provide employment for the enlarged population.[94] Sir John Sinclair estimated that by using new methods most Highland farms could be operated with only one-third of the servants formerly employed. Under the old agricultural system, plowing had required five men and five horses; with the English plow, one man and one horse did the same amount of work. When grazing areas were enclosed, herders were no longer needed.[95]   To be sure, new farms created in the drained swamplands absorbed part of the population, but that part was a small one.[96] In an attempt to alleviate unemployment, the government had encouraged linen manufacturing, but in the 1770's a depression struck that industry and the number of unemployed people in the Highlands continued to rise.[97]

The great number of idle people in the Highlands, frequently mentioned by contemporaries, lowered the standard of living and contributed new poverty to that which already existed.   Overwhelmed because of these conditions, many farmers, some of them evicted, sold the few animals and tools they possessed and, if they received sufficient money for passage, migrated to America.[98]   William Bain, a shopkeeper from Caithness, informed the port official in 1774 that he was going to Carolina because "the Poverty of the Common People with whom he dealt disabled them to pay their debts."[99]   Hector Macdonald, from Sutherland, a farmer seventy-five years of age, stated that he was going to America to make living conditions easier for his children, and, he added, "in all events they can scarce be worse."[100]   This poverty drove people to America in spite of the dangers of revolution in the 1770's. As late as September, 1775, a group of emigrants from Argyllshire, who expressed great loyalty to the House of Hanover, stated that they were willing to migrate to a rebel America since "it is better to confront an enemy in the wildest desert of that country, than to live like to beggars in their native land."[101]

Although idleness and penury had long been in the

Highlands, these were more potent forces for positive action when combined with the increase in information on idyllic America and with the removal of the clan structure, which had been a restraint to movement. Little wonder, then, that the poverty-stricken Highlanders read attentively the newspapers that assured them that:

The price of labour (from the scarcity of hands and great plenty of land) is high in the colonies: a day labourer can gain thrice the wages he can earn in this country. . . . There are no beggars in North America, the poor, if any, being amply provided for. Lastly, there are no titled, proud Lords to tyrannize over the lower sort of people, men being there more upon a level, and more valued in proportion to their abilities than they are in Scotland.[102]

CHAPTER IV

VOYAGE TO AMERICA

My country is ravag'd, my kinsmen are slain,
My prince is in exile, and treated with scorn,
My chief is no more—he hath suffer'd in vain—
And why should I live on the mountain forlorn?
                                    —from *The Jacobite Relics*.[1]

IN THE LAST half of the eighteenth century, the migration
of Highlanders to America proceeded in two major waves.
The first, beginning in 1749, was stemmed in 1775 by the
outbreak of the American Revolutionary War. At the end
of the war, a second wave surged toward the New World
and continued to bring Highlanders through the first half
of the nineteenth century. Within the confines of this
study, attention is centered on the first wave of migration,
1749-75. Although there was a constant movement of
Scottish Gaels to America during those twenty-six years,
the movement was greatly accelerated at the end of the
period, particularly after the Treaty of Paris of 1763.

The two waves of Highland emigrants can be dif-
ferentiated on the basis of leadership. From 1749 to
1775, the emigrant groups were organized and led by
tacksmen who were themselves forced to leave the Highlands because of economic and population pressures.
During the second wave, either the movements were

spontaneous or they were the result of promotion by ship agents.

Reports in periodicals of the departure of this first wave of Highlanders displayed one striking similarity—most accounts exclaimed at the wealth of the emigrants. The *Scots Magazine* typically referred to them as "persons of good circumstances," "the most wealthy and substantial people," or "people of property."[2] Only once were the departing described as poor people.[3] The *Edinburgh Evening Courant* revealed that in the fall of 1773 a ship left Fort William with 425 settlers who carried with them £6000 sterling. In November, 1773, the *Courant* estimated that 1500 Highlanders had left Sutherland for America in the two preceding years and had taken with them an amount larger than a year's rent for the entire country.[4] A gentleman from one of the Western Isles wrote in 1772 that emigrants from his island had taken with them at least £10,000. He lamented the loss of both the population and the money.[5]

While the periodicals of the time described the great wealth of those who sailed for America, British emigration records indicate that few of the settlers could be classified as wealthy. Many of the emigrants brought to North Carolina in 1774 by James Hogg could not pay their full fee for passage.[6] Travelers on the emigrant ships and colonial officials attested to the poverty of numbers of the migrants.[7] It appears that the periodicals of the day described largely the leaders of the movements in their emigration accounts. The tacksmen who organized the parties did frequently take large sums of money to America. The tenants, on the other hand, who made up the bulk of the movement, often had only money enough to pay for passage to America and arrived either penniless or with modest means.

For those who were emigrating, as we have earlier observed, funds were obtained from the sale of stock and agricultural equipment. Tacksmen, who traditionally had larger herds, departed for America with larger sums of money.[8]   Although many tacksmen were losing money during these years because of high rents and low cattle prices, they still had enough resources to settle comfortably in America.[9]   Allan McDonald, husband of Flora, brought his family to the New World in 1774 because of the threat of "poverty and oppression" in the Highlands, but after sale of his goods he had sufficient money to lease and operate a five-hundred-acre plantation in North Carolina—one of the finest in the upper Cape Fear area.[10] Accompanying the tacksmen and sharing the cost of transportation were those tenants who could secure sufficient funds to finance the voyage. The Highland Society at the turn of the century estimated that the average tenant could sell his stock and equipment for £10. Since the cost of transportation was usually about £3 10s. per adult and half that sum for children, the average tenant had enough money to secure passage for his wife, his two children, and himself.[11]   Cotters or subtenants could not migrate to America since, as day laborers, they had no property that could be converted into money.[12]

The genesis of an emigration and the process of organizing the groups composing it are two subjects worthy of consideration.   Before 1775, with few exceptions, the tacksman was the key to the emigration.   Having made his decision to move, the tacksman placed a notice on the church door publicizing his plans and inquiring if others in the parish desired to join him.   In some instances, several tacksmen agreed to leave together and jointly published their intent.[13]   James Hogg reported that he had no sooner announced his intention than he was be-

sieged by swarms of the discontented "cringing and fawn-
ing and begging" to be allowed to accompany him.[14]
Sometimes a meeting was held for all those interested and
the project was explained. Those who desired to join
the venture signed an agreement and made a payment
as token of their good faith. On one occasion 3000 people
joined such a group in a period of two days.[15] The tacksman then traveled to a port city and contracted with a
shipowner to transport the group. When transportation
costs were determined, each passenger was asked to pay
half of his fare so that the shipowner received half of
his money in advance. All money transactions were made
through the tacksman.[16] James Hogg, who brought 280
people from Caithness, Sutherland, and the Orkneys, asked
as a fee 1s. 6d. above the actual cost of transportation.
He received only about £12 for his labors, since many
did not pay him.[17] Hogg's remuneration was in fact small,
for other tacksmen asked 5s., 10s., and even 20s. for the
same services.[18]

The transportation contract between James Hogg and
James Inglis, Jr., the shipowner, has been preserved. This
document listed the ports of embarkation and debarka-
tion, set the transportation costs per person, specified what
provisions would be provided while at sea, and assigned a
£200 penalty for the failure of either party to fulfill the
contract. The tacksman and his family paid £6 per
person for what probably were cabin accommodations.
Hogg provided his own food. The other emigrants, who
had accommodations below deck and were fed by the
shipowner, paid transportation costs of £3 10s. for each
adult and half that sum for children under eight years.[19]

Margaret I. Adam describes the relationship between
the tacksmen and their tenants in terms of cruelty, ruth-
lessness, and exploitation on the part of the tacksmen.

She maintains that, when it was no longer possible to exploit the tenants in Scotland, tacksmen took them to America. There, in a frontier society, with neither property nor knowledge of the language, the tenants once more would be under the tacksman's control. Miss Adam suggests that the Highland tenants were willing to fall into such a trap because of "habits of obedience."[20] This picture of cruelty and oppression appears overdrawn. Some tenants, because of the kind treatment they had received, exhibited great attachment to their tacksman.[21] But, even if it be granted that the tacksmen were tyrants, it is not likely that tenants would voluntarily sell their property and follow their oppressors to America only to suffer further tyranny there. In addition, as will be noted in chapter VI, there is no evidence that tacksmen attempted to establish in America a feudal society in which they could continue to extract work services from the tenants and control them.

The tacksmen had legitimate reasons for guiding Highland groups to America. Often tenants and tacksmen were related and these blood ties resulted in genuine concern for the tenants. Also, as was noted above, the tacksman earned a certain sum of money by organizing an emigration group. This money paid part or all of his own transportation costs. The tenants, meanwhile, agreed to accompany him not because of the habit of obedience but because America was popularly believed to be the land of promise or because a tacksman assured them employment in the New World.[22] None of the Highlanders interviewed by British emigration agents in the years 1774-75 said he was migrating because of obedience or loyalty to his tacksman.[23] The struggling Highlanders followed the tacksmen to America because America offered economic relief and the promise of a golden future.

It was hope, not fear or obedience, that prompted the migration.

The tacksman provided a needed service in organizing the emigration. He had sufficient resources so that shipowners were willing to contract with him for the voyage. He had sufficient organizational ability to direct the movement. Once a pattern of emigration was established and Highlanders had become familiar with the techniques of organizing a group, they began to form emigrant companies without the leadership of tacksmen. This was the pattern after 1783. There is evidence for only one such spontaneous emigration before 1775 (from the Isle of Skye in 1771). Tacksmen had begun leading emigrant groups from this island as early as the middle of the eighteenth century. By 1771, the technique was well enough known that a party of 2000 organized themselves as a unit, complete with minister and surgeon, and made the necessary arrangements to emigrate.[24]

Eighteenth-century observers believed that the greatest emigration activity was in the Western Islands.[25] Analysis of the notices of departure to be found in contemporary sources seems to justify this opinion. Figure II indicates the number of emigrant parties identified as originating in each area.[26]

These reports are not complete because many departures from obscure places were not publicized, but on the basis of extant reports it appears that the two shires of Argyll and Inverness provided slightly more than half of the emigrant groups. These counties were also the most populous divisions of the Highlands. In each of the counties, the islands provided a sizable number of the emigrants. Perth, the large inland county, produced only one group. This may be explained in part by its greater distance from the sea and in part also by the tradition

FIGURE II. HIGHLAND COUNTIES FROM WHICH EMI-
GRATION PARTIES DEPARTED, AS REPORTED IN
CONTEMPORARY SOURCES

County	
Argyle	
Mainland	3
Islay	2
Jura	1
Kintyre Peninsula	4
Mull	1
	11
Caithness	2
Inverness	
Mainland	4
Skye	6
	10
Moray	1
Perth	1
Ross	
Mainland	1
Lewis	2
	3
Sutherland	5
Orkney Islands	4
Shetland Islands	1
Total	38

in that area of moving to the Lowlands instead of to
America.

A study of the ports of departure provides more information about the exodus. Port inspectors in Greenock,
Fort William, and Stromness have recorded the traffic from
their ports. Many emigrants boarded ships anchored off
the islands of Jura, Gigha, Islay, Skye, and Mull. Others

departed from such ports as Stornoway in Lewis, Thurso in Caithness, Loch Eribol in Sutherland, and Campbellton in Argyll. The frequency with which certain places were used as points of departure is recorded in port records as:[27]

Greenock in Renfrew	9
Fort William in Inverness	6
Skye	5
Stromness in the Orkneys	4
Gigha	2
Stornoway in Lewis	2
Islay	2
Jura	1
Loch Eribol in Sutherland	1
Thurso in Caithness	1
Dornoch in Sutherland	1
Kilkaldy in Fife	1
Port of Glasgow in Renfrew	1
	—
	36

The emigration movement reached its peak in the 1770's. Wherever they went, Boswell and Johnson in 1773 found people contemplating emigration.[28] The Reverend Alexander Pope in 1774 wrote that half of the people of Caithness would have left for America immediately if they could have obtained shipping.[29] The desire to migrate was reflected in the popular lyrics of the day and in ballads which proclaimed the glories of the New World. Farewell laments by emigrants were set to melodies and distributed from settlement to settlement.[30] On the island of Skye, in 1774, the inhabitants performed a dance called "America." "Each of the couples . . . successively whirls round in a circle, till all are in motion; and the dance seems intended to show how emigration catches,

till a whole neighborhood is set afloat."³¹   All ages were
captured in this emigration frenzy.   A company from
Strathspey in Inverness included "a woman of 83 years of
age, on foot, with her son before her playing *Tulluch-
gorum* on his bag pipes; some of them had children of
a month old, which the fathers carried on their backs in
a skull or wooden basket."³²

The departures of large numbers of Highlanders resulted in attempts by both individuals and the government
to stop the migrations.   Newspapers and letters in 1771
began to call for government action to halt this depopula-
tion.³³   That year, the Board of Trade turned down the
request of James Macdonald of the Isle of Skye and
Normand Macdonald of Slate for 40,000 acres in North
Carolina for settlement.   The request was disallowed because the Board of Trade felt that granting the request
would work to the disadvantage of the landed interests of
Scotland.   The Board announced its official position to
be one of encouraging the migration of foreign Protestants
to the colonies but of discouraging the migration of inhabitants of Britain.   The announcement of policy, however, did not prohibit the free movement of those who
desired to leave Scotland for America; and it did not stop
the granting of smaller plots to Highlanders arriving in
America.³⁴   Individual landlords sometimes attempted to
halt the migration.   After 840 of his tenants had departed
from the Isle of Lewis, Lord Fortrose, then living in London, hastened to Lewis to deal with his remaining tenants.
Asked the terms on which they would remain, the tenants
demanded revision of rents to the old rates and a refund
of the excess paid during the past three years.   The answer
of Lord Fortrose is not recorded.³⁵   Some landlords did
lower their rents to prevent the loss of all their tenants.³⁶
In spite of numerous demands, the government moved

slowly in shutting off the Highland emigration. A survey of the number leaving and their reasons for migrating was ordered in late 1773.[37] Emigration was finally halted in September, 1775, but only because the war had begun.[38]

It is impossible to determine the size of Highland emigration to America in the years 1730 to 1775 with any accuracy. Existing periodical accounts and government records are woefully incomplete. The best figures may well be the contemporary estimates. John Knox, writing in 1784, estimated that 20,000 Highlanders emigrated between 1763 and 1773. Thomas Garnett suggested in his *Tour*, published in 1800, that 30,000 left Caledonia between 1773 and 1775.[39]

Margaret I. Adam, in an attempt to test the above estimates, has surveyed the sailing notices in the *Scots Magazine* up to the year 1776. She found twenty sailings for America listed. She believes that the number of Highland emigrants in these groups was "something under 10,000."[40] An analysis of these twenty sailings does not confirm Miss Adam's computation. The *Scots Magazine* does list the departure of twenty parties of Highlanders for America.[41] Seventeen of the notices indicate specifically the number leaving. Adding these figures, the result is a total of 5804 departing between 1768 and 1775. The average group in the seventeen sailings contained 340 persons. If this average number is used for the three groups whose numbers are not specified, the total for the twenty emigrant parties is still only 6824, far short of the Knox estimate and short of the Adam estimate as well. However, the records in the *Scots Magazine* are not complete. The Port Records for 1774-75 showed the departure of nine groups of Highland settlers for North Carolina, while the *Scots Magazine* published notices of only two of the groups. The numbers printed in the *Scots Magazine* are round numbers, but they do not seem to be excessive. In the case of the James Hogg group, the *Scots Magazine* estimate was exact, but the Port Records were 150 short. If the *Scots Magazine* published news of only one-third or one-quarter of the sailings, as it seems to have done for the years 1774 and 1775, the number of Highlanders departing between 1768 and 1775 must have been more than 20,000. On this basis, the actual number would appear to be somewhere between the Knox and Garnett estimates, but probably closer to the latter.[42]

The voyage to America was a trying experience even under the best circumstances. The voyage was long— usually a month or two. Quarters, especially those below deck, were cramped and unventilated. Food became musty, moldy, or infested with vermin. Drinking water turned dark and strong.

There are reports that captains and shipowners added to the inevitable discomfort of the emigrants by breach of contract and even maltreatment. The Earl of Selkirk attempted to dismiss the troubles of the Highlanders aboard ship as seasickness.[43] However, accounts of three voyages to America substantiate the charges of mistreatment. Complaints center about the food provided for the passengers and the tyranny of the captains and crews.

In 1773 the brig *Nancy* left Dornoch in Sutherland with 200 settlers bound for New York. Of fifty children aboard under the age of four, only one survived the voyage. While at sea seven babies were born; all the mothers died and all the babies but one. Of the 200 who had embarked in Sutherland, only a hundred survived to see New York. The cause of this great mortality appears to have been the food which these emigrants received. In obvious violation of contract and in spite of the fact that an adequate supply of good food was aboard ship, the passengers were given only "corrupted stinking" water and an inferior, musty, black oatmeal "hardly fit for swine," which had to be eaten raw. By the time port officials in New York began examining the charges brought by the disembarked Highlanders, the ship had slipped out of the harbor.[44]

The *Jamaica Packet* made the voyage from Scotland to the West Indies and North Carolina in 1774 carrying settlers from the Orkney Islands. The settlers had been forced to leave the Highlands because of high rents. Crowded in a small compartment below deck, the passengers were once confined for a nine-day period during a sea storm. The compartment was ventilated only by the cracks in the deck above them, which also allowed the sea to run in when the deck was awash. According to contract they were to have received each week one pound of meat, two pounds of oatmeal, a small quantity of biscuit, and some water. The provisions actually supplied them consisted of spoiled pork, moldy biscuit, oatmeal, and brackish water. The passengers were fortunate to have potatoes, which were eaten raw and used to supplement their diet. For this fare and these accommodations, they were charged double the usual transportation fees because it was late October and all the other ships had gone when they arrived. Having only enough money for the regular charges, they were forced to sell themselves to the ship owner as indentured servants in order to pay for their transportation. Poorly nourished as they were and dreading the prospect of indentured servitude, the unfortunate passengers were set upon by the crew at the crossing of the Tropic of Cancer. On threat of dragging the emigrants behind the ship with a rope, the sailors attempted to extort the little property they still possessed.[45]

A historian of the Highlands has described the outbreak of smallpox and dysentery aboard the ship *Hector* on the way to America from Ross.   Eighteen children died and were buried at sea.   Contrary to contract provisions, the food was both scanty and wretched.   During the last days of the voyage, the passengers searched the ship's refuse for edible morsels.[46]

Thus, shipboard life, which was difficult at best for the mass of emigrants, was a terrifying experience for those on ships where contracts were not fulfilled.   Even aboard James Hogg's ship, the *Bachelor,* on which the passengers were provided with food rations of meat, meal, and biscuit twice as large as those on the *Jamaica Packet* and the *Nancy* and were furnished barley, peas, and molasses as well, eleven of 234 passengers died on the first leg of the journey to the Shetland Islands.[47]

When transportation conditions such as these were openly reported in the periodicals of the day, certainly some would-be emigrants were dissuaded by them.   The emigration probably would have been larger had life aboard ship been less trying.

Once in America, the Highlanders, preferring to live among those who spoke their language and shared their customs, usually settled in groups.   The largest settlements in North America were in North Carolina, New York, and Nova Scotia, but smaller groups settled in other colonies.

In the year 1735, a band of 160 Mackintoshes from Inverness migrated to Georgia.   They were recruited by James Oglethorpe to man the southernmost outposts of that colony against the encroachments of the Spanish. Under difficult conditions they colonized a strategic area and valiantly defended their new homes from Spanish attacks.[48]   Other small groups of Highlanders moved to Georgia, but the specific location of their settlement is not known. As late as December of 1775, a ship left the port of Stromness in the Orkneys bound for Georgia with people from Caithness aboard.[49]

Many Highlanders established themselves within the boundaries of colonial New York in the years before the American Revolution. As early as 1738, Lauchlin Campbell, from the island of Islay in Argyllshire, escorted thirty families to that colony. In the two succeeding years, he brought fifty-three families more, or a total of 423 people. The officials of the colony had promised Campbell 1000 acres of land, subject only to quitrents, for each family transported to New York. The greater number of these Highlanders received farms in Washington County.[50] Sir William Johnson, the superintendent of Indian affairs, was responsible for the migration of another group of Highlanders to New York. In 1773 Johnson brought 400 settlers to cultivate his lands in Tryon County, about thirty miles from Albany. These people, who were solidly Catholic, were largely Macdonells from Glengary, Glenmoriston, Urquhart, and Strathglass in Inverness-shire.[51] Besides these large groups, numerous small groups from Ross-shire, Sutherlandshire, and the island of Mull settled in New York.[52] Many of the New York Highlanders, like their kinsmen in North Carolina, showed Loyalist sympathies when hostilities developed between the American colonies and Britain. When the military tide began to turn against them, they fled to Canada in 1776 and in the following years.[53]

In the Nova Scotia area, the Highlanders did not begin their settlement until the 1770's. Although plans were laid for a settlement on Prince Edward Island in 1768, it was not until years later that the departure of 100 people to settle the island was reported.[54] The island became a haven for persecuted Catholics in 1772. John

Macdonald of Glenaladale in that year brought 200 of his co-religionists to America because of anti-Catholic feelings in South Uist.[55]   Other groups of Scottish Gaels arrived in the Nova Scotia area before 1775, but the settlement of Highlanders there did not become large until after the outbreak of war, when Loyalists from the revolting colonies fled to Nova Scotia for sanctuary.[56]

The Earl of Selkirk called the settlement of Highlanders in North Carolina the largest on the American continent, and his judgment appears to be correct.[57]   Of emigration notices in the *Scots Magazine* that mention destination, ten of the nineteen groups involved were bound for North Carolina, four for New York, three for Nova Scotia, and two for Georgia.[58]   It is this Highland settlement in North Carolina, the largest in America, that will be discussed in the following chapters.

CHAPTER V

SETTLEMENT

Where the copsewood is the greenest,
Where the fountains glisten sheenest, . . .
Hie to haunts right seldom seen,
Lovely, lonesome, cool and green,
Over bank and over brae
Hie away, hie away.

—from *Waverley*.[1]

ALMOST A century elapsed after the failure of Sir Walter
Raleigh's Roanoke Island colony in the 1580's before ef-
fective settlement of the North Carolina area was begun.
English promoters, neglecting North Carolina because it
was not easily accessible, had turned their attention to the
Chesapeake Bay region and the Charleston area.

Although North Carolina had an extensive system of
rivers emptying into spacious sounds—suitable geographic
features for colonization—most of her settlers came into
the colony overland from South Carolina, Virginia, and
Pennsylvania. This was true because the sounds (Albe-
marle, Pamlico, Currituck, Bogue, Core) were too shallow
and treacherous for safe navigation. Moreover, a sand
reef stretched for 300 miles along the coast to menace
naval traffic. The inlets to the sounds were part of this
shifting sand bank, and they, too, were unpredictable
and threatening. This natural blockade prohibited the

Map II. NORTH CAROLINA IN 1770

utilization of the Chowan, Roanoke, Tar-Pamlico, and Neuse rivers as avenues for settlement. In North Carolina, only the Cape Fear River proved navigable for seagoing ships, but it was not opened until about 1720.[2]

Political conditions also hampered the development of the colony. Carolina was originally conferred upon Sir Robert Heath in 1629, but he made no efforts to colonize the area. Following the Restoration, Charles II in 1663 granted the region (31 to 36 degrees of north latitude) to eight proprietors. The region was later divided into two separate political units—South Carolina and North Carolina. During the period of proprietary control (1663-1729), confusion and disorder engulfed the North Carolina government. The proprietary governors, some of whom were unusually inept and unscrupulous, were harassed, deposed, and even imprisoned by the unhappy inhabitants of the colony. Because of its chaotic political life, the colony received a bad reputation that further retarded settlement. With the royalization of the colony, government became more effective and the political scene more tranquil.[3]

Only the Cape Fear River provided a waterway into the colony, but it was rarely used until the 1720's. Sand bars at the mouth of the river prohibited ships drawing more than eighteen feet from entering.[4] Seagoing vessels as large as 300 tons were able to sail up the Cape Fear, however, and since most British seafaring vessels in the eighteenth century were smaller than 300 tons, the sand bars at the entrance to the Cape Fear were not a major impediment to use of the river.[5] The Tuscarora Indians residing in the area were not effectively subdued until 1715.[6] Moreover, during the second decade of the eighteenth century, pirates held the mouth of the Cape Fear as their base of operations, menacing river traffic until the

year 1718.[7] Finally, in 1724, the land office for the Cape
Fear region opened and settlement began along the river.[8]
It was in the upper reaches of the Northwest Cape Fear
River that the Scottish Highlanders began to settle in the
1730's.[9]

The date of the first settlement of Highlanders on the
Cape Fear was probably 1732. Before 1700, several Lowland Scots resided in the colony. The first governor,
William Drummond, and one of the early members of the
Council, Thomas Pollock, were both Lowlanders.[10] It has
been commonly believed that Highlanders were living in
the upper Cape Fear area as early as 1729, but there are
no documents to substantiate this claim.[11] Land-grant
records name James Innes (from Caithness), Hugh Campbell, and William Forbes as the first persons with Highland names to settle on the Cape Fear River. Innes is
registered as having received a grant of 320 acres in
Bladen County in January, 1732, and another of 640 acres
sixteen months later. Campbell and Forbes secured their
640-acre grants in April and May of 1733.[12] It was necessary for the grantee to be in the colony and personally to
"prove" his land rights (i.e., convince the "governor in
council" of his ability either personally or with family,
servants, or slaves to cultivate the acreage of land requested).[13] James Innes was appointed justice of the
peace in New Hanover precinct in November, 1734.[14]
Until proof is presented of the presence of earlier Highlanders on the Cape Fear River, this group must be
recognized as the first members of a colony that became
populous in the next forty years.

Governor Gabriel Johnston, who arrived in the colony
in November, 1734, traditionally has been given credit for
encouraging the Highlanders to settle in the province and
for bringing James Innes to it.[15] It is evident that Innes

worked closely with Johnston during the latter's term of office, 1734-52, but it is doubtful that Innes came to America because of Johnston.[16] According to records of the Board of Trade, the first notification of his appointment as governor of North Carolina reached Gabriel Johnston on March 27, 1733.[17] Innes had already been in North Carolina at least fourteen months when Johnston arrived. Although Governor Johnston probably was not involved in the migration of James Innes to North Carolina, he did promote immigration into the colony. In 1740, following the landing of a group of 350 Highlanders, the Governor supported a proposal granting newly arrived "foreign Protestants exemption from Publick or County" taxes during their first ten years in the colony. The sponsors of the bill stated that it was designed to encourage other Highlanders to come to North Carolina.[18]

Of the names to be found on the land-grant lists for 1732 and 1733, only three appear to be Highland names, but the group that came to North Carolina during those years may have been more numerous. This is intimated by the extensiveness of the grants which the three received. The records show that Innes was given three plots of 640 acres each, while Forbes received two plots and Campbell one plot of this same size. Under crown regulations at that time, land grants were made at the rate of 50 acres for each person (slave or free) brought into the colony.[19] Computed at this rate, the group must have consisted of approximately 76 people. Since slaves were late to arrive in the upper Cape Fear section, the group probably was made up of white immigrants.[20] Innes, Campbell, and Forbes may have agreed to transport this number (approximately 19 families) to America in return for several years of their labor. This hypothesis is made more plausible by the fact that grants were issued to numerous individuals with Highland names in the years 1734-37.[21]   At the end of several years of service, those who came as indentured servants under such a plan would have been free to claim land grants of their own.

On the other hand, the twelve new individuals who received grants in the years 1734-37 may have been part of another immigrant group encouraged to come to America by reports from the first group.   A certain Captain James Lyon received a grant in the spring of 1734, and he may have been part of another party of migrants, since it is not likely that he came to America under any type of indenture pact.[22]   The fact that those persons with Highland names who were given land in the years 1734-37 received such large plots seems to argue against the thesis that these individuals came as bound servants. The recipients of the smallest plots were John Smith, who was given 299 acres, and Neil Gray and Alexander Legg, who received 350 acres each.   All other grants to Highlanders in 1734-37 were for 400 acres or more.   Grants of 640 acres were made to six individuals.   It is quite possible, therefore, that those persons who received grants during the years 1734-37 were newcomers and not part of the group brought earlier by Innes, Forbes, and Campbell.

From the description of the land plots in the records of the Secretary of State, we can determine the location of the early settlement.   Those who received the first grants traveled upstream over 100 miles beyond Wilmington.   Hugh Campbell secured land on the Cape Fear River four miles above Rockfish Creek—this was only a short distance south of Cross Creek.   William Forbes and James Innes received lands on the Cape Fear twenty-two miles above Rockfish Creek.   Other grants were farther downstream, in an area 60 miles above Wilmington where

Hammond Creek drains into the Cape Fear River.[23] Interestingly, both Hugh Campbell and James Innes held land in the northern settlement and in the southern settlement as well. There is no ready explanation why the Highlanders should have chosen these scattered locations. In later years, the region near Rockfish Creek and Cross Creek was to become the center of the Highlander colony in North Carolina.

Coming from the chilly climate of North Britain, the Highlanders had to adapt themselves to a new and different environment in North Carolina. Since the Cape Fear settlement was at thirty-five degrees north latitude, summers were warmer and winters milder and shorter than in the Highlands. In the winter months, snows were less frequent. The fear of hurricanes felt by some newcomers was moderated by the knowledge that the storms did not usually do "much mischief."[24]

Colonial North Carolina (like the contemporary state) contained three distinct geographic regions—the Coastal Plain, the Appalachian Piedmont, and the Appalachian Mountains. The Coastal Plain stretched inland from the Atlantic Ocean more than 100 miles. On this plain the rise in elevation from east to west was hardly perceptible, averaging only two feet per mile. The sand hills in the region of the upper Cape Fear River were the most prominent relief features of the Coastal Plain. This was the section in which the Highlanders settled, an area of hills, short ridges, and undrained depressions bordering on the upper Cape Fear River and its tributaries.[25] The light soil of the Coastal Plain—chiefly clay and sandy loam—was productive because of abundant rainfall. While the sand hills themselves were not fertile, the many bottom lands in the sand hills region produced excellent crops of Indian corn and European grains.[26] The sand hills were covered with longleaf pine, a tree with a tap root long enough to reach the clay subsoil. It was from this tree that turpentine, rosin, pitch, and tar were extracted. During the eighteenth century, the products of this industry—naval stores—constituted the chief exports from North Carolina.[27] The fertile low regions between the sand hills were either canebrakes or thickets, heavily grown over with pea vines and other foliage. This was in contrast to the sand hills, which supported the pine trees but little undergrowth. English visitors who viewed the sand hills marveled at an area so fit for hunting. Since the sand hills had little undergrowth and since few longleaf pine trees had branches lower than twenty feet above the ground, it was possible for mounted hunting parties to gallop through the woods unhampered by the foliage and branches which slowed European hunts.[28]

Upon their arrival in North Carolina, the Scottish migrants disembarked either at Brunswick or Wilmington. Brunswick, the first town established on the Cape Fear River, was laid out in the mid-1720's. Although it became a port of entry and the seat of a customhouse, the community was slow to grow. One visitor in 1775 described it as "but a straggling village."[29] Since Brunswick was only twelve miles from the mouth of the river and since the major sand bars were seven miles above the town, ships could easily reach the port.[30] However, Wilmington, which developed in the latter part of the 1730's at the point of juncture of the Northeast Cape Fear and the Northwest Cape Fear, grew faster than its neighbor town sixteen miles downstream.[31] The two communities were, for a time, spirited rivals for the trade of southeastern North Carolina; by the Revolution, Wilmington (originally called Newton or New Town) had outstripped Brunswick.[32] Wilmington possessed several advantages. Being farther upstream, it was closer to the producers of naval stores and grain—the major exports. The area around Wilmington was more populous than the swampy region near Brunswick.[33] A third factor of great importance to Wilmington was the support of Governor Gabriel Johnston, who disliked the leading citizens of Brunswick and who promoted Wilmington to spite them.[34] Most eighteenth-century seafaring vessels could clear the shoals in the river, so Wilmington became the chief port on the Cape Fear River. Immigrant groups who were going inland welcomed the transportation farther upstream. Thus the contract between James Hogg and James Inglis, Jr. stipulated that passengers and cargo were to be delivered at Wilmington. This saved Hogg extra transportation expense.[35] Probably the Highlanders who arrived in North Carolina in the early 1730's landed at Brunswick. Later, although the people on large ships continued to disembark there,[36] most passengers went upstream to Wilmington to land.[37]

After landing at Wilmington or Brunswick, the new settlers still faced a laborious ninety-mile trip up the Cape Fear River to the Cross Creek area.[38] In order to continue up the river, the colonists at Wilmington were forced to transfer to "long boats, lighters, and large canoes."[39] This transportation was both slow and uncomfortable. A group of Moravians who rowed long boats up the Cape Fear considered that they made good time by averaging fourteen miles a day.[40] At this rate, the voyage up to Cross Creek must have required at least a week.

The next town above Wilmington was the hub of the Scottish settlement. It was situated on the banks of Cross Creek, a stream that emptied into the Cape Fear River from the west, midway between Rockfish Creek and the Lower Little River. The two branches of Cross Creek merged only two miles above the mouth of the stream. It is the tradition of the area that the creek received its name because people believed the two streams crossed without mingling.[41]   At this junction a town developed in the early 1760's, and it was known simply as Cross Creek.[42]

The colonial assembly labored in vain for almost a decade to determine the location of a proposed trading town on the upper Cape Fear River. A committee named in 1760 reported two years later that a suggested site at the mouth of Rockfish Creek was inaccessible from the back country, and a location at the fork of Cross Creek was too far from the Cape Fear. The committee found that the best location was on Cross Creek only a short distance from the Cape Fear.[43]   Six years later the committee report was acted upon by the assembly, and a bill was passed to establish a town called Campbellton on the site selected. To encourage merchants and settlers to establish themselves there, Campbellton was named seat of the court for Cumberland County.[44]   The assembly, however, had acted too slowly. When the committee was just beginning its investigation, lots in a proposed town of Cross Creek were already being sold. By 1768, eighty-four lots had been purchased, and it is likely that a flour mill had been constructed. In the town of Campbellton, located a mile and a quarter away, only eight lots were sold by 1768.[45]   Cross Creek grew to be a busy trading center, but eighteenth-century Campbellton, which had the endorsement of the Assembly, was never more than a small residential area with a courthouse.

The great concern of the colonial assembly to establish a trading town on the upper Cape Fear resulted from the isolation of the newly settled North Carolina Piedmont region. Rivers draining the Piedmont flowed into South Carolina, and exports from that section were usually sold in Charleston, or less frequently in Virginia.[46] To reduce the dependence of Piedmont settlers on other colonies and to channel their trade through North Carolina merchants, the Assembly built roads to the Cape Fear from Orange County (1775), from the Catawba River (1763), and from the Dan River in northern North Carolina (1773).[47] All of these roads ended in the Cross Creek–Campbellton vicinity and were important avenues of trade. Map III shows the trade routes in the Colony.[48]

The first large group of Highlanders to make its way up the Cape Fear and settle in the Cross Creek area was a party of 350 from Argyllshire who disembarked in September, 1739. As with many migrations after the Forty-five, this group was led by members of the Highland gentry. In February, 1740, two of the leaders appeared before the Colonial Council asking special consideration for "themselves and several other Scotch Gentlemen and several poor people brought into this province."[49] In response to the needy condition of many of the newly arrived Highlanders and in order to encourage other Highlanders to follow them, the upper house passed a bill, described above, granting "foreign Protestants" release from tax payments for their first ten years in the colony. In addition to this, the bill requested that £1000 of the public money be given to "Duncan Campbell, Dugald McNeal, Daniel McNeal, Coll. McAlister and Neal McNeal Esqrs to be by them distributed among the several families."[50] The lower house agreed to the tax relief, but deferred action on the £1000 dole.[51] When the council met again in June, 1740, parcels of land were granted to this group. The leaders appear to have claimed large

Map III.   NORTH CAROLINA TRADE ROUTES IN 1770

plots of land on the basis of the headrights of those whom they had brought to America. Duncan Campbell alone received 2643 acres. Although this immigrant party consisted of 350 persons (eighty-five or ninety families), only twenty-two individuals received land grants. (See Figure III.[52]) All land granted was along the Cape Fear River, and most of the plots were on a section of that stream between Cross Creek and the Lower Little River in Bladen County.[53]

The Cross Creek region, which had been part of New Hanover County in 1733, was in Bladen County in 1739. The constant stream of new settlers entering North Carolina frequently made it necessary to subdivide large frontier counties and to add new counties. The formation of counties in the Cape Fear section is recorded in Map IV.[54] New Hanover County (originally known as a precinct) was established in 1729, embracing all the land drained by the Cape Fear River. Five years later Bladen County was formed from New Hanover County. It extended from the junction of Livingston's Creek and the Cape Fear as far northwest as the headwaters of the Cape Fear.[55] In 1750 Anson County was laid out in the area just north of the South Carolina line, west of Drowning Creek, and south of the Granville line.[56] Cumberland County, the county in which most of the Highlanders resided, was not established until 1754. Beginning a short distance south of Rockfish Creek, Cumberland County extended north to the Granville line, east to Drowning Creek, and west to South River.[57] Ironically, the county probably was named after William Augustus, the Duke of Cumberland, second son of George II, who was known to the Highlanders as "Butcher Cumberland." Lacking evidence, one can only speculate whether the Highlander

Figure III. LAND GRANTS TO NORTH CAROLINA
HIGHLANDERS IN JUNE, 1740

Name	Acres	County
James McLachlen............	160	Bladen
Jas McLachlen..............	320	"
Jas McLachlen..............	320	"
James McLachlen............	320	"
Duncan Campbell............	150	"
Duncan Campbell............	75	"
Duncan Campbell............	320	"
Duncan Campbell............	300	"
Duncan Campbell............	140	"
Duncan Campbell............	640	"
Duncan Campbell............	320	"
Duncan Campbell............	150	"
Duncan Campbell............	400	"
Duncan Campbell............	148	"
James Campbell.............	640	"
Patric Stewart.............	320	"
Dougal Stewart.............	640	"
Arch McGill................	500	"
James Fergus...............	640	New Hanover
Arch Douglass..............	200	"
Arch Douglass..............	640	Bladen
Col McAlister..............	320	"
James McAlister............	640	"
James McDugald.............	640	"
Hugh McCraine..............	500	"
Gilbert Pattison...........	640	"
Jno McFerson...............	320	"
Dan McNeil.................	105	"
Dan McNeil.................	400	"
Daniel McNeil..............	320	"
Dan McNeil.................	400	"
Neil McNeil................	150	"
Neil McNeil................	400	"
Neil McNeil................	400	"
Neil McNeil................	321	"
Hector McNeil..............	300	"
Arch Campely...............	320	"
Arch Bug...................	320	"
Murdock McBraine...........	320	"
Alex McKey.................	320	"

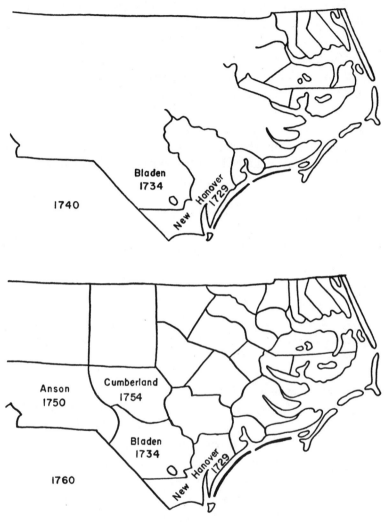

MAP IV. FORMATION OF COUNTIES IN
THE CAPE FEAR BASIN

inhabitants of the area were consulted concerning the choice of the name.

The rate and size of this Scottish immigration into North Carolina are as difficult to determine from the colonial side as from the home side. Only fragments of the Port of Brunswick Record Book remain, and there is no complete record of the arrival of ships in the Cape Fear section. Other sources sometimes speak of the landing of Highlander immigrant parties, but fail to speak of the numbers involved. All of the groups of Highlanders arriving before 1776 whose numbers have been recorded are listed in Figure IV. From their location in the Port of Brunswick Record Book, it appears that groups 3, 4, and 5 in Figure IV reached America in 1773 or 1774, but since the date set down there has been obliterated, this cannot be definitely affirmed. For the years 1768 through 1772 there is a paucity of specific information on the arrival of groups of Highlanders, in spite of the fact that during those same years the *Scots Magazine* mentioned the departure for North Carolina of groups totaling 1930 individuals.[58] The letters of Governors William Tryon and Josiah Martin substantiate the size of the migration described in the *Scots Magazine*. Governor Tryon wrote to the Earl of Hillsborough in March, 1771, that 1600 settlers from the islands of Arran, Jura, Islay, and Gigha had settled in the colony during the previous three years. He added that most were residing in Cumberland County.[59] Governor Martin reported on March 1, 1772, "Near a thousand people have arrived in Cape Fear River from the Scottish Isles since the Month of November with a view to settle in this Province whose prosperity and strength will receive great augmentation by the accession of such a number of hardy laborious and thrifty people."[60] From this evidence it is clear that the migration of Highlanders brought many new settlers to North Carolina, although the size of the settlement is, of course, no more accurately known than the rate of immigration.[61]   Governor Martin, when planning the uprising of Loyalists in 1776, estimated that an army of "much greater numbers" than 3000 could be raised among the Highlanders.[62]   This opinion was also shared by some of the leaders of the Highlanders.[63] The military potential of a population was considered at the ratio of one soldier for each group of four inhabitants.[64] The colony of Highlanders, therefore, may well have numbered 12,000.   This is obviously a rough estimate.

Since the influx of Scotsmen commenced shortly after the royalization of the colony in 1729, the disposal of unclaimed lands was the responsibility of crown officials. According to Board of Trade regulations, the governor, in consultation with the council (i.e., the "governor in council"), authorized grants of lands.[65]   Instructions to the first royal governors specified that persons desiring plots were to appear before meetings of the "governor in council" to prove their right to obtain land.   But the infrequency of council meetings and the inconvenience of traveling long distances to attend them obstructed the land-granting process and encouraged squatting.   To make land more available to the people, Governor Gabriel Johnston and his council in 1741 delegated the power to prove land rights to the several county courts, where the inhabitants "could more conveniently attend and the number of the Familys could be more easily known."[66] The new settler, after finding a plot of unclaimed land, appeared with his family (servants and slaves included, if he had any) at the meeting of the county court.   When the findings of the court were submitted to the governor's secretary, a warrant for the appropriate number of acres in the given county was issued.   The precinct surveyor,

FIGURE IV. ENUMERATED HIGHLAND GROUPS THAT
ARRIVED IN NORTH CAROLINA BEFORE THE REVOLUTION

Date of Arrival	Ship	Highlanders Aboard	Place of Embarkation	Former Home	Source
1. Sept., 1739.	—	350	—	Argyllshire	C.R., Vol. IV, pp. 489-490.
2. Nov. 4, 1767.	—	50	Isle of Jura	Isle of Jura	C.R., Vol. III, pp. 543-544.
3. ——	—	102	Greenock	—	P.B.R.B.
4. ——	—	244	Isle of Skye	Isle of Skye	P.B.R.B.
5. ——	—	228	Isle of Skye	Isle of Skye	P.B.R.B.
6. 1774.	Bachelor of Leith	280	Thurso	Caithness and Sutherland	S.M., July, 1774, p. 345; N.C.H.R., April, 1934, p. 130.
7. Oct. 17, 1774.	Ulysses	91	Greenock	Argyllshire	N.C.H.R., January, 1934, p. 51.
8. Fall of 1774.	Diana	34	Greenock	Kintyre in Argyllshire	N.C.H.R., April, 1934, p. 142.
9. Dec. 1 ——	Cato	312	Isle of Skye	Isle of Skye	P.B.R.B.
10. Jan. 17, 1775.	Carolina Packet	62	Greenock	—	N.C.H.R., April, 1934, p. 129.
11. Oct. 21, 1775.	George	172	—	—	C.R., Vol. X, pp. 324-328.
12. Nov. 12, 1775.	Jupiter of Larne	130	—	Argyllshire	C.R., Vol. X, pp. 324-328; N.C.H.R., April, 1934, p. 138.
		2055 Total			

Sources: C.R.—*Colonial Records of North Carolina.*
N.C.H.R.—"Records of Emigrants from England and Scotland to North Carolina, 1774-1775," *North Carolina Historical Review,* XI (January and April, 1934).
P.B.R.B.—Port of Brunswick Record Book (a fragment of a sheet), from Angus McLean MSS.
S.M.—*Scots Magazine.*
Items 3, 4, and 5 are incomplete because of mutilation of P.B.R.B.

upon receiving the warrant, marked out the stated number of acres on the chosen plot and returned a description of the site to the auditor's office. After the payment of fees and the routine approval by the "governor in council," the settler received a land grant.[67] The grant read as follows:

George the Second by the Grace of God of Great Britain France and Ireland King Defender of the Faith &c

To all to whom these presents shall come—Greeting

Know ye that we for and in consideration of the rents and return therein reserved have given and granted and by these presents for us our Heirs and successors do give and grant unto ————— a Tract of land containing —— Acres of land lying and being in the County of ————— in our Province of North Carolina ————— as by the plot hereunto annexed doth appear together with all woods waters Mines minerals Hereditaments and appurtenances to the said Lands belonging or appertaining (one half of all Gold and Silver mines excepted) to hold to him the said ——— Heirs and assigns forever as of our Manner of East Greenwich in our County of Kent in free and Comon Sockage by Fealty only yielding and paying to us our Heirs and assigns forever the yearly rent of Four Shillings proclamation money for every hundred acres hereby granted to be paid to us our Heirs and successors on the second day of February in each Year at such places in our said Province as our Governour for the time being with the advice and consent of our Council shall think fit to direct and appoint provided always that in case the said ——— Heirs and Assigns shall not within the space of three years after the date hereof clear and cultivate according to the proportion of three Acres for every hundred; and also that if a minute or Docket of these our letters patent shall not be entered in the Office of our Auditor General for the time being in our said province within six months from the Date hereof that then and in either of the said cases these our Letters patents shall be void and of none effect. In testimony whereof we have caused the Great Seal of our said province to be hereunto affixed Witness our trusty and well beloved Gabriel Johnston Esqr Our Captain General and Governour in Chief at ———— this ———— day of ———— in the ———— Year of our reign Anno Domini.[68]

There were, of course, abuses in the granting of lands. It was a policy to grant a "right" to a person each time he entered the colony. One colonist, James Minge, crossed the border of the colony six times and his slave, Robin, crossed it four times. Minge then claimed ten head rights.[69] Some grantees stretched their grants along the river, thus monopolizing the rich bottom lands. This practice ceased after royal surveyors were ordered "to take care that not above one fourth part of the land granted shall border upon the river, that is . . . there shall be four chains in depth backwards for every chain in front."[70] In North Carolina there were few grants of large plots of land to English speculators. Those large grants that were made were granted by the Board of Trade, not by North Carolina officials. It is true that Henry McCulloh, a relative of Governor Johnston, held three grants totaling 190,000 acres.[71] This was, however, contrary to the usual crown policy. The Board of Trade instructed the royal governors to disallow single grants larger than 640 acres.[72] North Carolina was a colony of small landholders.

While the new settler could, if he had sufficient resources, buy an acreage from an earlier settler, he could not purchase land from the crown.[73] During the period of their control, the proprietors had sold land subject to smaller quitrents than those required for land granted on the basis of headrights,[74] but the crown made no such arrangement. Royal officials granted land free, subject only to a small surveying and transfer fee, and collected the same quitrent from all—four shillings proclamation money per hundred acres. Land in North Carolina was never held in fee simple; quitrents were always demanded. For the newly arrived Scottish settler with few resources, the quitrent system was ideal. Those former Highland tenants who sold livestock and tools in order to pay the costs of migration often had little money left upon their arrival in America. In North Carolina the Highlander could secure a grant of land on the basis of headrights and his fees, at the most, amounted to only £1 sterling.[75]

Not all Highlanders were able to receive land grants immediately. Some came to America as bound servants and served a term of years in return for their transportation.[76] Others came penniless and could not afford to pay land grant fees or purchase the tools and animals necessary to build a shelter and begin farming.[77] A few came as tradesmen seeking work, not land.[78] For these reasons, a study of the land grants received by North Carolina Highlanders yields important, although not complete, information about the size and character of the upper Cape Fear settlement.

Fortunately, the land grant records in the office of the North Carolina Secretary of State in Raleigh are "nearly complete" for the colonial period and in a good state of preservation.[79] These records show that 691 persons with Scottish Highland names received land grants from the crown in the years 1732 to 1775. Included in the records is information on the size, date, and area of the grants. Some Highlanders, of course, purchased land outright from other settlers and did not receive land grants. In order to determine the total area of settlement, I secured from county records information on land purchases. Courthouse fires in Bladen and Anson counties have destroyed all records for the pre-Revolutionary period, but for Cumberland County—the county in which most Highlanders resided—the land transfer records for the colonial period are extant. These records list all land sales from the formation of the county in 1754 to the Revolution. During this span of years, 312 persons with Scottish Highland names purchased land in the county. Of this total number, 146 bought land from other Highlanders, while 166 bought land from non-Highlanders. Figures V and VI indicate the number of land grants and land purchases secured by Highlanders each year.

During my examination of the colonial land records, it became necessary to develop a method of selecting authentic Highland names. There were Scotch-Irish settlements both to the east and to the west of the Highlanders, and in these settlements many names commonly considered as Highland names appeared. For example, the Campbells and McKays were leading families in both the Highlander settlement and the Scotch-Irish settlements. The Scotch-Irish colony to the east of the Highlanders was small and apparently did not cross the South River. For that reason, it was arbitrarily decided to consider only grants west of the South River in this study. On the other hand, the region west of the Highlanders between the Pee Dee and Catawba rivers was so heavily populated by these people it became known as "Scotch-Irish Mesopotamia." Some of the Scotch-Irish moved east of the Pee Dee River on Mountain Creek, Falling Creek, and Marks Creek, mixing with Highlanders in the same area. For this study, in order to be reasonably sure of excluding Scotch-Irish names, it became necessary to set an arbitrary line east of the mixed settlement. Accordingly, Highlanders established on Naked Creek, Drowning Creek, Gum Swamp Creek, or Joes Creek were included, but the few Highlanders living on the eastern tributaries of the Pee Dee were not included in this study. Another com-

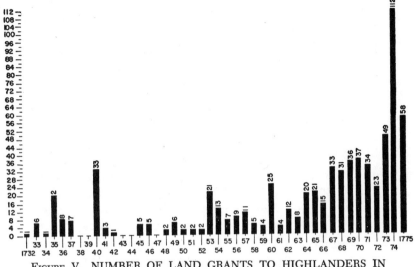

FIGURE V. NUMBER OF LAND GRANTS TO HIGHLANDERS IN
THE CAPE FEAR AREA, BY DATE

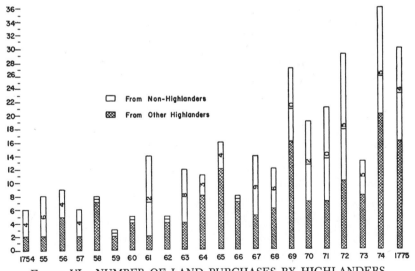

FIGURE VI. NUMBER OF LAND PURCHASES BY HIGHLANDERS
IN CUMBERLAND COUNTY, BY DATE

plication was the presence of English, Welsh, and Lowland Scot settlers within the area of the Highland colony. In order to avoid mistakes in the identification of the Highlanders, three categories were established. Category one, "Highlanders," is made up of the 123 persons clearly named in the *Colonial Records* and in the "Emigration Records for 1774-1775" as emigrants from the Highlands. Category two, "Probably Highlanders," includes all those bearing family names mentioned in category one. Thus, Murdock McBraine is in category one, and all other McBraines not specifically mentioned on migration lists are in category two. Several names such as Gilchrist, Frazier, McNair, and Munn, which are clearly Highland names, were, although not present in category one, added to category two.[80] Category three, "Possibly Highlanders," contains many names such as Shaw, Brice, Dunn, McAlexander, or Lyon, which may be either Highland or Lowland names. Many inhabitants of the southern Highlands, particularly Argyllshire, had names common in the Lowlands. Persons placed in category three usually received grants at the same time and in the same area as people in the above two categories. Individuals in category three also normally have Christian names used by Highlanders. In Figures VII and VIII, land grants and land sales are broken down into the three categories. As these figures indicate, the third category does not involve more than one-third of the names used. A complete list of the names in the three categories appears in the Appendix.

Figure V shows that before 1753 the Highland migration was sporadic, with new groups receiving land in 1733, 1735, 1740, and 1753. The only one of these emigrations concerning which evidence (besides land grants) is available is the one that occurred in 1740, when the

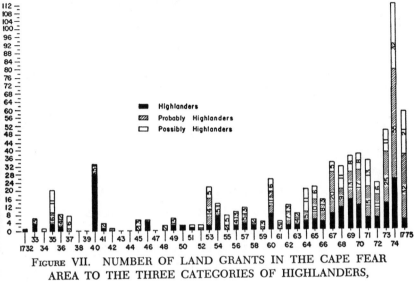

FIGURE VII. NUMBER OF LAND GRANTS IN THE CAPE FEAR
AREA TO THE THREE CATEGORIES OF HIGHLANDERS,
BY DATE

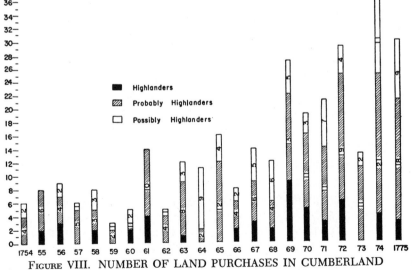

FIGURE VIII. NUMBER OF LAND PURCHASES IN CUMBERLAND
COUNTY BY THE THREE CATEGORIES, BY DATE

immigrants appealed to the legislature for tax relief. The few grants in 1736 and 1737 were made to some who received plots in 1735 and to others who probably were part of the 1735 group, but who, for some reason unknown to me, did not receive grants the first year. Likewise, in 1741 and 1742, additional grants were made to persons who were part of the large 1740 group. There was no sizable influx immediately after the defeat of the Highlanders in the Forty-five; instead, the year 1747 shows a decrease in grants. During the French and Indian War, the granting of land continued, and the figures of 1760 probably mean that a large group entered the colony. There was a gradual increase in the number of grants in the late 1760's and the early 1770's until the peak was reached in 1774. It is significant that the rising tide of emigration described in the *Scots Magazine* from 1768 to 1774 is reflected in the rate of land grants.

The record of land sales in Cumberland County as depicted in Figure VI shows the same increase as does the graph of land grants, with 1774 as the peak year. The most striking difference between the two graphs can be seen by a comparison of the years 1760, 1761, and 1772. Figure VI indicates, as could be expected, that the number of land purchases rose as the Highlanders became more numerous. However, the relationship between the immigration rate and the level of land sales was not necessarily a direct one, since it appears that many land purchases were made by the older Highland settlers who had earned sufficient money to make such investments.[81]

Unfortunately, it is impossible to determine positively the number of newly arrived Highlanders receiving grants or buying land in any given year. Such statistics, if they existed, would be a better guide to the rate of immigration. The statistics on land grants used here include many duplicate grants. Sometimes individuals received three, four, or five separate grants. Under Board of Trade regulations, if an individual settled on his plot and cleared the specified number of acres, he could receive another grant of land on the same terms. The only limit on the land-granting process was the individual's ability to till the land and pay quitrents. A further complication is the fact that many Highlanders had the same names. Favorite Christian names appeared again and again in the same families. The first federal census returns for Cumberland County in 1790 show seven Daniel McLaines, four Archibald Brices, five Daniel Morrisons, and six Neal McNeals, all of whom were heads of families.[82] If the number of dependents holding those names were added, the list would be much larger. In the 1790 census returns, in fact, Highland names that appear only once are few in number. Among the Highlanders, identification was assured by the use of nicknames. To differentiate between the several Hector McNeals, one was called "Bluff Hector," since he lived on a high bluff overlooking the Cape Fear; and another, because of the color of his hair, was known as "Red Hector."[83] Since land records, of course, do not use these nicknames, it is difficult to detect duplication of names or to determine dates of initial land grants or purchases.

In Figure VI, Highlander land purchases in Cumberland County are divided into purchases from other Highlanders (in the three categories mentioned) and purchases from non-Highlanders. This indicates that approximately half of the land purchased by Highlanders was obtained from non-Highlanders.

A study of the land grants to Highlanders shows that over 60 per cent of the plots acquired were between 50 and 200 acres in size. Grants of 640 acres were more frequent among the early settlers in the 1730's and 1740's than among those who came just before the Revolution. This may indicate that the later settlers came over as individuals and secured smaller plots, while the earlier groups of Highlanders were under some obligation to tacksmen, who were able to obtain larger plots on the basis of group headrights. Of the 691 land grants, only one was for more than 640 acres. This was a grant in the year 1749 for 1000 acres.[84] It was clearly contrary to the Board of Trade policy for the "governor in council" to make a grant of that size.

By approximating the location of the 691 land grants and the 312 land purchases on a map of the Cape Fear area, the progress of the settlement can be roughly traced year by year. With few exceptions, all grants were located either upon or close to rivers, since waterways were the chief avenues of transportation. In the late 1760's and the 1770's, a few grants were located on the roads built into Cross Creek. The index books in the office of the Secretary of State establish locations with reference to rivers, creeks, trees, stumps, or rocks. The brief entries are sometimes picturesque, but rarely are precise enough to give an exact location. The following are typical examples: "North east of the N. W. River at the fork of Hugh McCranes Creek," "on Upper Little River," "on Slap Arse Swamp," "about a mile South of Rockfish."[85] Maps V-VIII were not intended to give an exact picture, but only to suggest an approximate pattern of the process of settlement before the Revolutionary War.

In making the maps in this work, the eighteenth-century maps by Collet and Mouzon were used to determine the names of the major streams and the locations of towns and wagon roads. In a few instances, small streams which existed in the eighteenth century have disappeared

Map V. LAND GRANTS AND PURCHASES SECURED BY
HIGHLANDERS, 1733-1745

and there is no way now to determine their exact locations.
In such cases, the land grant or purchase is placed on
the larger stream into which the smaller and now unknown stream emptied. On this basis, grants on Buck

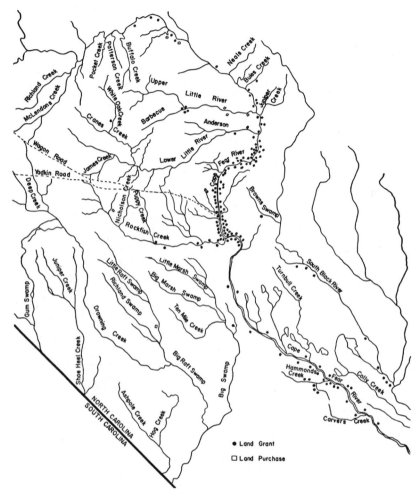

MAP VI. LAND GRANTS AND PURCHASES SECURED BY
HIGHLANDERS, 1733-1755

Creek were placed on Deep River; Lock and Resucks
Creek were added to Flat Creek; and Tranthams, Duck,
and Hugh McCranes Creek were placed on the Cape
Fear River in northern Cumberland County.[86]

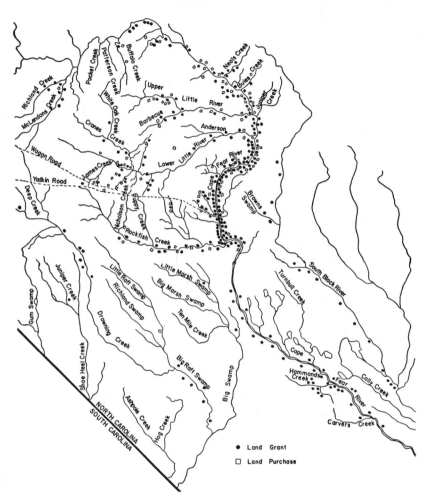

MAP VII. LAND GRANTS AND PURCHASES SECURED BY
HIGHLANDERS, 1733-1765

Maps V-VIII show that the main regions of settlement
were along the Cape Fear River, Upper Little River, and
Rockfish Creek—in that area which today comprises Cumberland, Harnett, and Hoke counties but in the eight-

MAP VIII. LAND GRANTS AND PURCHASES SECURED BY
HIGHLANDERS, 1733-1775

eenth century was all Cumberland County. Although a
few Highlanders established themselves in the Hammond
Creek area to the south during the early years of settlement, they did not become numerous in this region. By

1753 the pattern of settlement to the north along the Upper and Lower Little Rivers had been set. When the population became heavier in this section, some colonists moved north to till the lands on Deep River. Others went west to Drowning Creek and Joes Creek. Some moved beyond Drowning Creek into Anson County, but their area of settlement cannot be easily determined because of the Scotch-Irish in that region.

Thus, by 1775, a large body of Highlanders was situated along the rivers in the sand hills region of the upper Cape Fear. Because land was plentiful and they had come from an agricultural society, the majority of Highlanders became farmers in North Carolina.

CHAPTER VI

LIFE ON THE CAPE FEAR

Ye shall hae barley bannocks store,
Wi' geese and gaizlings at your door;
A good chaff bed upon the floor,
If you'll marry me, my dearie, O.
—from *Ancient Ballads of Scotland*.[1]

FOR THE Highlanders, disembarkation in North Carolina marked the beginning of a new life. Of course, in the Cape Fear settlement Gaelic was spoken, some relatives and friends were near, and certain Highland customs persisted, but the changes were nevertheless many and great. The new climate and terrain required many adjustments. To exploit the soil, different agricultural methods had to be learned and new crops planted. Since the Scots were moving into a frontier area, homes had to be built and lands cleared before the normal pursuits of the planter could begin. In the midst of a struggle for physical existence, these immigrants reestablished the church they had known in the Old World, took part in a new political system, and adapted themselves to the language and living habits of the non-Highlanders about them. For many who before 1745 had lived under the protective custody of the tribal system, the migration to America constituted the final step to personal independence, since in America the Highlanders wrestled with nature and shaped a new society with neither the help nor the protection of clan and chief.

The economic activity in which most North Carolina Highlanders engaged was agriculture. There were merchants, clergymen, tailors, and shoemakers, too, but the overwhelming majority of the Highlanders cultivated either their own land or the land of another. The Scots normally arrived in the fall or early winter and began working on their acreage as soon as the land was surveyed. The season in which they arrived was determined by several factors. By departing from Scotland in the fall, the tenants received the benefits of the year's crop. By arriving in North Carolina in early winter, the immigrants came at a time of plenty, could secure an acreage to be tilled the following year, and had sufficient time to adapt themselves to the climate before the summer brought "fluxes, fevers and agues."[2]

Having secured a survey of his chosen plot, the new settler proceeded to fell enough longleaf pines to build a shelter for the family. In the area thus cleared, he usually constructed a log home chinked with clay, although clapboard houses appeared with greater frequency after the sawmills were built.[3] The settlers cultivated the land lying along the streams and put stock to graze in the back areas.[4] Preparing land for cultivation did not involve cutting down more trees. The colonists killed a tree by removing a ring of bark, which caused the trees to drop their foliage and allowed the sun to reach the crops. An English traveler exclaimed at the ominous appearance of the fields filled with dead trees, and he marveled that the planters were seldom hurt by falling trees or branches.[5]

Because of the obstruction of roots and trees in the fields, planters found it difficult to use plows.[6] Although both Neil Buie and Archibald McKay had plows in the 1760's,[7] most planters employed hoes both to turn over the soil and to weed it later. The high cost of transportation made farm tools expensive and highly prized.[8] The simplicity of the agriculture can be seen in the inventories of estates at that time. Typically, farmers used only such equipment as a knife, a hammer, a saw, several horseshoes, an ax, an ox chain, a spade, a saddle, a cart, shears, several iron wedges, several hoes, and a basket or tub.

In the fields prepared for cultivation, the settlers planted Indian corn, wheat, oats, peas, beans, flax, or sweet potatoes.[9] One observer noted that the usual rotation of crops in North Carolina was corn (two or three years), beans or peas (one year), and wheat (two or three years). He reported corn yields of from sixty to seventy bushels per acre and pea and bean yields of thirty to forty bushels.[10] The soil produced well at first but was exhausted shortly. The settlers did not attempt to restore the fertility of the soil through grasses or manures. Land was so plentiful that it was easier to abandon the old field and prepare a new one for cultivation.[11] Because land was so available, the European technique of fertilizing soil was forgotten by some Americans. A Scotswoman visitor to the colony reported that her sister-in-law, a planter's wife, was shocked at the mention of manuring land. The woman declared she would "never eat corn that grew thro' dirt."[12]

Some settlers built mills on their land both for their own use and to provide a source of income. In 1736, the governor and colonial council issued a proclamation that the construction of a sawmill in the Cape Fear section would be sufficient for maintaining title to a 640-acre grant without any cultivation of the land.[13] Both gristmills and sawmills were needed by the new settlers.

Governor Dobbs reported to the Board of Trade in 1764 that forty sawmills had already been erected on the branches of Cape Fear.[14] John Campbell constructed a mill on Buffalo Creek, and Hector McNeil by 1761 had built two mills (a gristmill and a sawmill) on his plantation near Cross Creek.[15] After the Revolution, Allan McDonald requested compensation from the British government for his gristmill in Anson County that had been seized by the rebels. He valued the mill at £120 and added that in the past its yearly income had "Keeped the whole Family in Bread."[16]

The simplest form of enterprise for those who were new in the colony was animal husbandry—raising horses, cattle, and hogs. Since there were no fences, not even around some cultivated fields, the stock roamed about freely in search of food.[17] This system of open grazing made wills written at this time indefinite about the number of stock possessed. Jeane Campbell's will divided between two persons "What horses I have in the woods."[18] The inventory of Neil McNeil's estate, a document one would expect to be exact, refers to "some wild horses in the woods" and "a stock of hoggs about 30 heads."[19] Planters attempted to keep the stock tame and near home by putting out salt for them once a week.[20] The cows returned to the plantation yard each evening when the calves were penned up.[21] In early summer, there was customarily a roundup, and it was at this time that the owners branded their calves and enclosed cattle to be sold. Brands were registered with the colonial authorities.[22] The system of common grazing areas was not new to the Highlanders; it was the method of grazing used in North Britain before the advent of the enclosure movement.[23] About the size of these herds, the author of *American Husbandry* reported to his English readers that herds of cattle up to 2000 head were not uncommon in North Carolina.[24]   The few inventories of estates of Highlanders now available show herds of 36, 27, 15, 22, 30, and 10 head each.[25]   Loyalist claims, which were sometimes inflated, indicate that some Highlander farmers owned large numbers of livestock.   Daniel Ray claimed ownership of 8 horses, 40 cattle, and 100 hogs in 1776. Soirle Macdonald testified that when he fled his plantation he left behind 7 horses, 53 cattle, and 264 hogs.[26]   Cattle and hogs to be sold usually were driven to Charleston.[27] The size of the cattle sent to market is not known, although a record survives of one Daniel Paterson who drove a cow that weighed 1000 pounds to Charleston.   The "black cattle" which were raised in the Scottish settlement normally weighed considerably less than 1000 pounds when marketed.[28]   Some cattle and hogs were butchered in the Highlander settlement and the meat placed in barrels and salted.   The casks were then moved down the river to Wilmington on flat boats and finally reached the West Indies for sale there.   However, competition from Pennsylvania and scarcity of salt in the upper Cape Fear area curtailed this meat-exporting enterprise.[29]

It is well known that during the eighteenth century North Carolina exported more naval stores than any other colony.[30]   Since the Highlanders lived in the region of the longleaf pine, it might be expected that they were among those who produced tar, pitch, turpentine, rosin, masts, and spars.   But evidence that any of them did take part in that economic activity is by no means clear. The inventory of the estate of Thomas Rutherford, who lived just south of Cross Creek, seems to show that he produced ninety-three barrels of tar, which were sold to a Wilmington merchant.[31]   If Rutherford could produce tar, then his Highlander neighbors may have done so too.

To this point, all that has been said about the economic activity of the planters has referred to those who held their own land either through grant from the crown or direct purchase from an earlier settler. There is a paucity of information about the large number of Highlanders who did not possess their own land. The author of *Informations Concerning the Province of North Carolina* provides one source of knowledge about those Highlanders who had insufficient funds to pay the land-grant fees and to purchase the necessary tools and stock to begin farming. According to this source, large holders assigned portions of their lands to these poor Highlanders, who became tenants. The owner supplied the necessary tools and livestock. In return, the tenant paid the owner, yearly, one-third of the crops produced and one-third of the increase of the livestock.[32] The wills of Andrew Armour (1792) and Neil Buie (1761) seem to indicate that they were members of the tenant class. Both possessed livestock and were active planters, but they did not have land to bequeath to their children.[33] Buie's inventory of estate showed that he owned only ten cattle and one horse. These animals probably constituted his share of the increase of the herd provided by his landlord. Because of his limited circumstances, this tenant could give four of his daughters only one shilling each, one daughter a cow, and his two sons the remaining animals to be divided between them.

Besides the Highlanders who secured their own plantations and those who became tenants, there was yet a third category of immigrants. These came as indentured servants. In return for their transportation to the New World, they were bound to serve their employers for a set period of years. There is no evidence on which an estimate of the size of this group can be based. The census of 1790 listed only twelve indentured servants in the homes of Cumberland County Highlanders.[34]   The Revolutionary War had halted immigration for eight years, and the Scots were reluctant to move to North Carolina in the 1780's because of the treatment afforded Loyalists. The figure for 1790, then, was probably abnormally low. The term of indenture for Highlanders varied from three years to five years.[35]   After 1741, the freed servant received £3 proclamation money and a suit of apparel. Moreover, he could then qualify for a land grant on the basis of headrights.[36]

Although slaves were not so numerous in the inland counties as on the seaboard, Cumberland County had a relatively large number of them. In the 1760's the wills of Highlanders show that they were among the owners.[37] The lists of taxables for 1756, sources subject to suspicion, indicate that there were 302 whites in Cumberland County and 74 Negroes.[38]   The first federal census in 1790 provided reliable statistics on slaveholding. There were in Cumberland County 717 slaves owned by people with Scottish Highlander names.[39]   The Highlander population of the county in 1790 was 2834; the ratio of slaves to Highlanders was therefore one to four. For North Carolina as a whole in that year, the ratio was 2.8 whites to each Negro.[40]

Approximately one-fourth of the Highland families had slaves, and among those Highlanders who held slaves the average number of slaves per family was 4.7.   In the counties of Warren and New Hanover, where larger plantations were located, the average was 10.3 slaves per slaveholding family. On the other hand, in Randolph County, west of Cumberland County, the average was 3.5. It has been noted that the ratio of Cumberland Highlanders to the slaves in 1790 was four to one.

The number of slaves held by Cumberland Highlanders varied widely, though one-third of the Highlander slave-owners possessed only one slave. The census returns for 1790 provided names of the large slaveholders. Farquard Campbell had 50 slaves, William Gordon 17, "Coll" McAlister 15, Alexander McAlister 40, Archibald McDuffie 13, John McLean 41, Archibald McKay, Jr., 19, and Archibald McNeil, Sr., 30.[41] The fact that numerous Highlanders held slaves, and held them as early as the 1760's, gives credence to the statements of the *Scots Magazine* that the migration was led by men of "wealth and merit" and that it was not merely an exodus of the exploited poor.[42]

Fortunately for the newcomer, a benevolent nature made easier the task of feeding his family. A variety of fruits, berries, and grains were available to those who would harvest them. Mulberries, persimmons, plums, cherries, brambleberries, raspberries, Spanish figs, and a grain called "wild corn or rye," all grew wild. Grapes, however, were the most plentiful fruit. Both blue and white grapes flourished on the bottom lands and the uplands.[43] On some small streams grape vines grew up the trees on either bank and finally arched the creek. One visitor described a pleasant boat excursion during which the delighted passengers looked up to discover clusters of succulent grapes "dangling over our heads."[44] Wild meat was also plentiful. Rabbits, turkeys, partridges, pheasants, wild ducks, and geese abounded. Bear meat was considered "very wholesome" by the Highlanders' Moravian neighbors, who thought bear fat "as good as olive oil" with salad.[45] Deer were prized since they provided venison and deerskin to clothe the settlers as well.[46] In the rivers and streams the colonists found perch, pike, and rockfish.[47] In these ways, the forests, streams, and uncleared fields gave valuable assistance to the colonists attempting to subsist in the New World.

Most of the Highlanders engaged in agriculture, as we have seen; a few of these Scottish planters also had other occupations. John Campbell was, in addition, a surveyor; John Clark, a tailor; Angus McDugal, a weaver; Neil McNeil, a shoemaker; Allen Cameron, a millwright; and Patrick McEachin, a blacksmith.[48] In Scotland many Highlanders had combined another craft or occupation with agriculture. For example, some Highland tenants were also fishermen, kelp burners, weavers, or tailors.[49] When they came to America, they brought their skills and were ready to carry on activities other than farming.

A few of the Highlanders in North Carolina became merchants. Fortunately, the Gaelic colony had developed in an area that needed a trading town. The settlers of the upper Cape Fear and nearby Piedmont area required a closer center where they might dispose of their surplus and purchase needed articles. Cross Creek, which was located on a branch of the Cape Fear River and was served by two roads from the west, filled the need. Three gristmills there converted grain from the back country into flour and meal.[50] Cattle and hogs were slaughtered. Merchants also purchased such varied items as hides, lard, lumber, barrel staves, and tar, and these products, along with the meat and grain, were floated down to Wilmington on log rafts.[51] The merchants returned in boats with merchandise to be sold to the settlers. Among the products in demand among the colonists were needles, buttons, thread, buckles, silk, nutmeg, salt, pepper, molasses, rum, powder, and iron products such as hinges and hoes.[52] As the instrument of this exchange, the merchant played a valuable role in the economic life of the section.

The development of Cross Creek can be traced in the

Records of the Moravians in North Carolina. As roads were built to the town and as more merchants established themselves there, the Moravians transferred their business from Charleston to Cross Creek. In 1772, the Moravians began sending monthly messengers to the town for the Wilmington paper.[53] Trade with Cross Creek had begun in 1765,[54] but it was not until 1773 that the Moravians sent many products there for sale. According to a Moravian record book for December 10, 1773, "Br. [Brother] Bagge took only four wagons to Charleston this time, for recently the stores in Cross Creek have improved, so that he secured several wagon-loads of goods from there, though as yet there is a poor assortment to select from, and little chance to dispose of the chief product of this country, that is hides."[55] When the Cross Creek merchants improved their stocks in the 1770's, they received much of the trade that had previously gone to Charleston. It was reported that forty or fifty wagons daily entered the town with agricultural products to be traded or sold.[56] During the early stages of the Revolutionary conflict, there was a salt shortage in the colony. Cross Creek apparently had a great store of that scarce commodity, for it continued to be sold there when it could not be secured elsewhere. In December, 1775, the Moravians were still able to purchase seven wagons of salt.[57] After the defeat of the Highlanders at Moore's Creek Bridge, all salt stores at Cross Creek were seized and divided among the victorious soldiers, and many of the merchants were taken prisoner and put in Halifax jail. But only a month after the battle, the Moravians who went to Cross Creek found that "the stores there were nearly all open, and goods were willingly and gladly sold; all was quiet and peaceful. . . . The shopkeepers who were taken to Halifax town were released on security, and were looking after their stores again."[58]

Highlanders were prominent among the merchants of Cross Creek. Those most active in the town were William Campbell; Robert Gillies; James Hogg, acting as an agent for his brother's firm of Hogg and Campbell; Neil McArthur; Clark and McLeran; Robert Donaldson and Company; and Bachop and Patterson.[59] For shrewd merchants, profits were high. Neil McArthur came to Cross Creek in 1764 with only a little property, but by 1775 he reported he was worth over £4600.[60] Although merchants ordinarily carried a wide variety of goods, one Highlander in Cross Creek was a specialist. Murdock McLeod, a surgeon and apothecary, sold only medicines.[61]

The population of Cross Creek was not predominantly Gaelic. The records of sales of lots from 1760 to 1775 show that only twenty individuals with Highlander names bought lots in the town, while 144 non-Highlanders purchased lots in the same period. In nearby Campbellton, the Highlanders bought only one lot during the 1760-75 period.[62] Thus, although the Highlanders were represented in Cross Creek and some were prominent men in the town, Cross Creek was a settlement largely of non-Highlanders. Most of the Highlanders preferred to live on plantations and to earn their livelihood through agriculture.

The Highlanders who came to North Carolina were Presbyterians, and they built churches of their denomination in the colony. There is no evidence of Highlanders in other churches in the upper Cape Fear area. Although there were regions of North Britain that remained Catholic or Episcopalian in the last half of the eighteenth century,[63] most areas either were or became Presbyterian. The religion of the Lowlands spread through the north mainly as a result of the effective work of the Presbyterian Society for the Propagation of Christian Knowledge.[64]

Many, if not most, of the North Carolina Highlanders were from Argyllshire; and Argyllshire was overwhelmingly Presbyterian by 1750 (4000 Catholics and 62,000 Presbyterians).[65] Duncan Campbell, one of the leaders of the group of 350 that migrated to North Carolina in 1739, returned to Argyllshire in 1741. The minutes of the Presbytery of Inverary for November 3, 1741, reveal Campbell's concern for the religious welfare of the colonists:

There was a representation at this time laid before the Presby. by Duncan Campbell of Kilduskland for himself and the Argyle Colony settled at Capefair in North Carolina shewing their earnest desire of having a minister soon settled among them, who is a person of merit and of an unblemished character, because the Gospel is yet in effect to be planted in those parts where there is a considerable number from our bounds already settled and a prospect of a great number of the poorer sort to follow and who are in deplorable circumstances for want of Gospel ordinances there being but two or three ministers in the whole province and these of a poor character, who besides have not the language spoke. . . .[66]

Because the prospects of receiving an adequate "sallary" in North Carolina were "inconsiderable," Campbell found it impossible to secure a Gaelic-speaking minister. He petitioned the Presbytery and the Society to provide the first year's salary for the transportation of the clergyman to America. The Society granted £21 for the project, but for unknown reasons a minister was not sent. The colonists were without a permanent pastor until 1758.[67]

The first Presbyterian minister to visit the Highlanders was Hugh McAden, an itinerant preacher to the Scottish and Scotch-Irish settlements of North Carolina. McAden's journal indicates that on Sunday, January 25, 1756, he arrived at the home of Hector McNeil (probably Bluff Hector, who lived on the Cape Fear a few miles above Cross Creek) and preached to a group of Highlanders.

Since the minister was Scotch-Irish and did not speak Gaelic, he suspected that some of the people present had not understood a single word of his sermon. After an unfortunate attempt to sing the psalms, McAden acknowledged that the Highlanders were "the poorest singers I ever heard in all my life." Traveling fourteen miles the next day to the David Smith plantation north of the Lower Little River, the preacher spoke to a gathering of settlers from that area. Another meeting was held on Thursday at the home of Alexander McKay on the Yadkin Road— near the location where Longstreet Church was later built. Here he preached to a congregation of people, mostly Highlanders, who appeared highly pleased with his message. However, when the Scots remained at the McKay home all night long drinking and shouting profanity, McAden decided their former expressions were "feigned and hypocritical."[68]

In October, 1758, the Highlanders contracted for the services of their first minister, the Reverend James Campbell of Pennsylvania. According to tradition, Campbell, a native of Argyllshire, came to North Carolina after hearing of the religious needs of the Cape Fear Scots from Hugh McAden.[69] It was agreed that Campbell receive yearly "a hundred pounds in good and lawful money of North Carolina."[70] Twelve men in the community signed the agreement with the minister, making themselves responsible for payment of the salary.[71] Since the Anglican Church was the established church in North Carolina, dissenting ministers were required to sign a test oath. James Campbell attended the January term of court in Cumberland County, in 1759, and subscribed the following: "I, James Campbell, do declare that I do believe that there is not any transubstantiation in the sacrament of the Lord's Supper, in the elements of bread and wine at or after the consecration thereof by any person whatsoever."[72] Because of the existence of the established church, Campbell and other dissenting ministers could not legally perform marriage ceremonies before 1762.[73] Even after that date there were restraints—the fee for the service was always given to the pastor of the Church of England in that parish and banns could not be announced for dissenter weddings.[74] Campbell was able to serve his Scottish parishioners, however, freely and effectively. Under his leadership, the Highlanders founded at least three churches.

Since the Highlanders were dispersed over a wide area, they could not attend one church. The Reverend James Campbell served the several congregations on alternate Sundays. One congregation met in "Rogers Meeting House," a simple structure near Roger McNeil's plantation and only a short distance from Hector McNeil's bluff on the Cape Fear. Alexander McAlister, Farquard Campbell, Hector McNeil, and Duncan McNeil served as elders of the church. A second church was built about 1765 on Barbecue Creek. This church ministered to the needs of the people residing on both the Upper and Lower Little Rivers and their immediate tributaries. While Flora McDonald lived at Cameron's Hill, she attended the Barbecue Church. The elders of Barbecue Church, noted through the settlement for their piety and knowledge of doctrine, were Gilbert Clark, Duncan Buie, Archibald Buie, and Daniel Cameron. Members of a third congregation continued for several years to meet in the home of Alexander McKay, as they had when Hugh McAden came to preach to them. About the year 1766, this congregation also constructed a meetinghouse, called Longstreet Church. The church was so named because of its location on the Yadkin Road. In this church, Archibald Mc-

Kay, Archibald Ray, and Malcolm Smith served as elders. Although most of the members of the churches were Highlanders, enough other settlers attended to make it necessary for Campbell to preach sermons in both English and Gaelic each Sunday.[75]

Campbell labored along until about the year 1770, when the Reverend John McLeod arrived in the colony with a group of immigrants. He may have been part of the group that left the Isle of Skye in 1771 with "a parochial preacher and a thoroughbred surgeon."[76] Campbell and McLeod jointly ministered to the Highlanders until the outbreak of the Revolution, when both were forced to flee. McLeod, a Tory, joined the men under General Donald McDonald and fought with the Loyalist army at Moore's Creek Bridge. After being captured and imprisoned for a short time, the minister was released by the Patriots on condition that he leave the colony. He complied immediately.[77] Campbell, on the other hand, was an ardent Revolutionary Patriot who left the Highlanders at the outset of the war to minister to the Scotch-Irish in Mecklenburg and Guilford counties. One account of his leaving describes an incident after a service at Barbecue Church, when a Gael named Munn threatened to shoot Campbell should he again publicly pray for the success of the rebels.[78] The fruitful seventeen-year pastorate of James Campbell came to an end because of political differences with his fellow Highlanders. It may be said that the religious organization of the Highlander settlement was due almost entirely to his efforts.

The society at the head of the Cape Fear River was not composed entirely of Scottish Gaels. Approximately half of the inhabitants were from other areas of Europe. Although Highlanders constituted the largest national group, records of the time reveal the names of English,

Irish, Welsh, German, Lowland Scottish, and even French settlers residing in Cumberland County. Some indication of the size of the non-Gaelic population can be seen in the Cumberland records of land transfers. During the years 1754-75 some 1435 sales occurred, but Highlanders[79] were involved either as buyers or sellers in only 572 transactions (i.e., 40 per cent).[80] Two petitions that circulated within the boundaries of the Highlanders' settlement have been preserved in the *Colonial Records of North Carolina*.[81] On both petitions, over 50 per cent of the names were those of non-Highlanders. To be sure, the Highlanders were among the first to settle the upper Cape Fear section, and they came to constitute the largest national group in the area. It is doubtful, however, that they ever numbered many more than 50 per cent of the population.

Within the colony of North Carolina, the Highlanders were surrounded by other national groups (see Map IX).[82] To the south, along the mouth of the Cape Fear, were the large plantations owned mostly by English settlers. East of the Highlanders, groups of Welsh, Scotch-Irish, Swiss, and a small company of Irish migrants had established themselves. To the north, above the Haw River, another English settlement was located. Both north and west of the Highlanders were the mixed settlements of Germans and Scotch-Irish.[83] These surrounding peoples traded in Cross Creek, and in time a few did settle within the areas of Bladen, Cumberland, and Anson counties. Records of land transfers show that the Gaels continually bought land from and sold land to the non-Highlanders.[84]

The language barrier did not prove to be a serious handicap for the Highlanders. Samuel Johnson noted when he made his tour of the Highlands that the tacksmen, lairds, and ministers could speak English.[85] We know

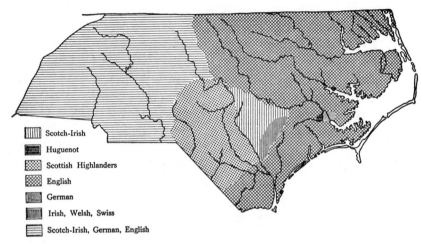

MAP IX. NATIONAL GROUPS IN NORTH CAROLINA IN
THE EIGHTEENTH CENTURY

such leaders in the North Carolina settlement as Farquard
Campbell and Alexander McAlister spoke and wrote
English,[86] and probably all the other prominent Highlanders in the colony did, too.   In the Highlands in the
eighteenth century, the Society for the Propagation of
Christian Knowledge established and operated the schools,
and instruction in them was in English.   As a consequence,
all educated people knew English.[87]   Moreover, those who
learned informally to read used English, for there was
little printed in the Scottish dialect of Gaelic.   Not until
1767 did the New Testament appear in that language.[88]
In North Carolina, contact with English-speaking neighbors and the use of English in some church services made
the language more familiar to the Gaels.   But in spite of
schools and books and church, the common people, in
North Carolina, as in North Britain, continued to use
Gaelic.   Some of the slaves in North Carolina homes also

adopted the language. Charles W. Dunn tells of the surprise of a newly arrived Highland lady in this regard.

As she disembarked at the wharf, she was delighted to hear two men conversing in Gaelic. Assuming by their speech that they must inevitably be fellow Highlanders, she came nearer, only to discover that their skin was black. Then she knew that her worst foreboding about the climate of the South was not unfounded and cried in horror, 'A Dhia nan fras, am fas sinn vile mar sin?' (O God of mercy, are we all going to turn black like that?)[89]

Gaelic was used by descendants of the first settlers far into the nineteenth century. The last Gaelic sermon in North Carolina was preached in 1860.[90] The language today is virtually unknown to those who live along the upper Cape Fear.

Highlanders displayed much interest in education. James Innes set aside £100 in his will "For the Use of a Free School for the Benefite of the Youth of North Carolina."[91] Although Innes owned property near Cross Creek, he came to reside near Wilmington. After his death, the executors of his estate organized Innes Academy in Wilmington.[92] Of the twenty-two wills made by Cumberland County Highlanders which are in the State Archives at Raleigh, half were made by people who could not sign their names. Malcolm Blue, one of those who used his mark to sign his will, in 1764 bequeathed "the sum of Eight pound prok. to my four youngest children to get them school."[93] Patrick Campbell, who could write, ordered in his will of 1775 that all his possessions not specifically given to anyone else "Be appropriated for the Schooling and Raering the Children."[94] It is not clear where Blue's or Campbell's children received schooling. It is highly possible that James Campbell, the minister, acted as schoolteacher during the week, since other Presbyterian ministers in North Carolina were serving in that dual capacity.   In Guilford and Mecklenburg counties, the Reverend David Caldwell and the Reverend Joseph Alexander were as much noted for their pedagogic activities as for their preaching.[95]   In 1774, Aeneas Mackay, a lad of twenty, who reported that he could read, write, and cipher, left Caithness on a ship bound for North Carolina.   Mackay said he was going to that colony as a teacher because of encouraging letters from Highlanders there.[96]   Apparently the Highlanders were looking for schoolteachers in the 1770's, as they earlier had solicited a minister from their homeland.

There were no known attempts on the part of former clan leaders to re-establish the clans in America.   The only instance of one man exercising authority over or leading a group of those from his own clan occurred in 1776, when Donald McDonald convinced many other McDonalds to rise against the North Carolina Patriots.   But, since the Highlander army raised in 1776 contained members from many other families, his move cannot be considered as an attempt to re-establish the clan system.[97]

The arrival of Flora McDonald in the Cape Fear settlement was an event of great importance.   She was a symbol of Highland bravery and independence—one of the most noted Highlanders to emerge from the Forty-five.   Following receptions at Wilmington and Cross Creek, the McDonald family moved to a plantation on Barbecue Creek, where other McDonalds had settled earlier.[98]   In January, 1776, Allan purchased a 475-acre plantation in Anson County on Mountain Creek which they named "Killegray."[99]   Unfortunately for the McDonalds, they arrived at the beginning of the Revolution.   They were to play a leading part in the raising of a Loyalist army.[100]   Zealous Patriots forced Flora to leave her new plantation only a few months after settling there. The McDonalds' stay in North Carolina was short and unpleasant. Allan, taken prisoner at Moore's Creek, was exchanged for a captured American officer after lengthy negotiations.[101] Flora and her children left North Carolina under a flag of truce after spending only four years in the colony.[102]

In spite of plentiful land and a bountiful nature, life in North Carolina was difficult for the new Gaelic settler, particularly if he arrived without financial resources. For some, the problems began immediately after disembarkation. One sea captain in 1769 deposited a shipload of Highland migrants in Virginia instead of North Carolina. The marooned emigrants had no money to travel the rest of the way to their intended destination. They reached North Carolina only after the Virginia legislature voted to provide food and transportation for their trip to the Cape Fear.[103] Similarly, when a group of "100 and odd Scots" arrived at Brunswick in 1767 without any money, Governor Tryon was forced to use £15 of the public funds for relief and assistance to the group.[104] Governor Martin, in 1772, welcomed the Scots as a fine addition to the colony.[105] Three years later Martin wondered if they could subsist in America. In March, 1775, he wrote to the Earl of Dartmouth, "Surely, my Lord, the Scotch Landlords are much wanting in their own interest if not humanity in expelling so many wretched people from their country who were useful there and who will perish many of them here before they can learn to live."[106] Combined with the many difficulties of making a living on a frontier plantation was the further problem of illness. Particularly in the low and swampy regions, "fevers" were common. The eighteenth century applied the term "fevers" principally to typhoid fever, yellow fever, and malaria.[107] A Moravian who visited Cross Creek returned

to Salem in 1766 with news of much illness in Cross
Creek.[108]   The *Moravian Records* show that, in 1770, a
woman who was traveling up the Cape Fear to join the
Moravian settlement stopped at Cross Creek, contracted
"the so-called Yellow Fever," and died.[109]   Highlanders
who spent lonely nights isolated in tiny cabins built in an
area thickly populated with wolves, wildcats, and snakes,
probably felt the same horror which John MacRae expressed in his poem, "Duanag Altrium":

> Tha sinne 'n ar n-Innseannaich cinnteach gu leoir;
> Fo dhubhar nan craobh cha bhidh aon againn beo,
> Madaidh-allaidh us besidean ag eibheach's gach groig.
> Gu'm bheil sinne 'n ar n-eiginn bho'n threig sinn
>   Righ Deors.

We've turned into Indians right enough; in the gloom of the
forest none of us well be left alive, with wolves and beasts
howling in every cranny.   We're ruined since we left King
George.[110]

The New World brought gifts, but it also brought new
difficulties and dangers.

Most of the settlers appear to have been below the age
of forty on their arrival in the colony.   James Innes was
in his early thirties[111] and "Coll" McAlister and Farquard
Campbell of the 1739 company were probably even
younger, since they were still enumerated in the 1790
census.[112]   The records for a group of thirty families who
left from Caithness indicate that the average age for heads
of families in this group was thirty-eight.   There were,
however, a remarkable number of older immigrants.   The
company from Caithness included John Catanoch, 55;
Aeneas McLeod, 60; James McKay, 60; Alexander Morison, 60; William McDonald, 71; and Hector McDonald,
75.   The average age of the settlers was lowered by the
many children who came.   On the Emigration Lists for

1774-75, a little more than half those numbered were children. For a total of 83 families, the average number of children per family was 2.1.[113]

In an age of many early deaths, the Highlanders frequently remarried. Two years after the death of James Innes, his widow married her husband's former business associate and settled at Point Pleasant, the plantation Innes had given her.[114] Farquard Campbell was widowed twice and married three times. His last wife, who was much younger than he, had been born aboard the ship on which he returned to North Carolina from a visit in Argyllshire.[115] The same disparity of age appears in the marriage of William McDonald, mentioned above as being in the group from Caithness. When McDonald came to America, the seventy-one-year-old man brought along his wife and three small children.[116] John McFarland, who died in 1767, apparently expected his wife to remarry. In his will he provided for his "Loving wife" by instructing his executors to purchase a slave woman to serve her "Duren hir Widdohood and at hir Marrage Winch and the Neagro fello Neamt Sam . . . sould and their Price Eackley Devidded Among^t the . . . Children."[117] Patrick Campbell also considered the eventuality of his wife's remarriage and her possible neglect of his children. His will provided that she could use his plantation only "During her Widohood or as Long as She Behaves Well to My Children to be Judg By My Exeutors."[118] Women could and did hold land and carry on farming. When Hugh Campbell died in 1736, his wife Magdaline continued to operate his large holdings on the Cape Fear and secured another 640-acre grant.[119] Women often received land grants: Mary Buie acquired title to 100 acres in 1769; Catherine McNeil was granted 400 acres two years earlier; Alexandra McAlister received 75 acres in 1771.[120]   Alexander MacAlister bequeathed his home plantation to his daughter Isabelle and gave a son only 5s.[121]   This will was unusual because most Highlanders continued the policy of male primogeniture, particularly regarding the home plantation.[122]

The Scottish colonists furnished their home simply. Because of the great distance from manufacturers and the difficulty and expense of transportation, they possessed a minimum of furniture and personal effects.   The women prepared and served the food with several iron pots, an iron ladle, a flesh fork, a knife, a trammel (adjustable pot hook), fire tongs, a griddle, pewter dishes, knives, and forks.   Larger pieces of furniture such as tables, chairs or stools, and chests were frequently homemade and crude. The settler family also had feather beds, blankets, several spinning wheels, and a pot rack.[123]   The fullest information on clothing is contained in the inventory of the estate of Neil Buie.   The list included "2 jackets, 2 britches, 1 pr trowsers 1 pr stockings 1 bonnet a handkerchief . . . 1 pair of garters . . . a silver broach 2 shirts."[124]   Those who came to America with wealth, of course, had greater possessions.   John Brown held title to only 200 acres in Cumberland County, but his inventory of estate noted such luxuries as "2 smoothing irons and 1 looking glass."[125] Archibald Clark's inventory listed "1 pair of silver buckles 1 stock buckle 1 pair sleve butons . . . 1 Bible—3 other books five Catechism . . . 17 gallons of rum . . . 1 drinking glass.[126]   Other Highlanders kept large stores of liquor in their homes; Soirle MacDonald reported 200 gallons of brandy seized at his home by Patriots after the Battle of Moore's Creek.[127]   Allan McDonald was among the wealthiest people in the colony.   His Loyalist claim for compensation stated that furniture, books, and silver plate worth

£500 fell into the hands of those who plundered his estate.[128]

When living conditions of the Highlanders who remained in Scotland are compared with those of the settlers in North Carolina, several important differences are apparent. In both places, of course, there were wealthy and poor, with great contrasts in housing, from gloomy dens to commodious manors. The Highland tacksmen in Scotland lived stylishly. Isabel F. Grant described the typical home of an eighteenth-century tacksman in these words:[129]

There were probably a mahogany table and leather-seated chairs, both in the dining-room and in the drawing-room, and the latter may have some 'pire glasses,' and perhaps 'sewed work footstools.' There would have been an imposing four-post bed with steps and curtains in the family bedroom, and smaller beds with 'damity' curtains for the guests and grown up children. . . . The kitchen would be very generously supplied with 'sass pans,' spits, a ham kittle, a candle-making machine, and other utensils. There were two or three small carpets for the floors, and prints and 'family picters' on the walls.

Samuel Johnson did not think the tacksmen's homes as luxurious as those of similar gentry in England. He found the homes and the furniture were "not always nicely suited." After an excellent meal, he was escorted by his host to his bedroom where he discovered "an elegant bed of Indian cotton, spread with fine sheets. The accommodation was flattering; I undressed myself, and felt my feet in the mire. The bed stood upon the bare earth, which a long course of rain had softened to a puddle."[130] Janet Schaw, who visited North Carolina in 1774, found a similarly incongruous situation there. She was entertained in the home of an unnamed Cape Fear planter whom she described only as a "Gentleman." She found his home well-furnished, with an excellent library including fine globes, a telescope, and "Mathematical instruments." The meal was served on china and silver, but Miss Schaw described the house itself as "little better than one of his Negro Huts."[131]   Allan McDonald, who was "embarrassed in his affairs" in Scotland, brought to America over £1000 and ultimately settled in Anson County. He purchased a plantation of 475 acres, of which seventy acres were already clear. On the plantation were a fine home, three orchards, barn, storehouse, kitchen, stable, corn crib, and gristmill. McDonald brought five indentured male servants and three indentured female servants to perform the agricultural and domestic work of the plantation. He valued the furniture, books, and silver in the home to be worth £500.[132] The lengthy inventory of the estate of Mrs. Jean Corbin (Mrs. James Innes) suggests that wealthy Highlanders in America had homes as well-furnished as those in Scotland.[133] The many items in her inventory included:

> 14 Silver Knives
> 20 do (ditto) forks
> 2 Diamond Rings
> 6 Punch Bowls
> 8 Looking Glasses
> 5 Mahogany dining Tables
> 12 Leather bottom'd Chairs
> 1 Backgammon Table
> 12 Large Table Cloths

There appears to have been some improvement in the living conditions of the tenant-class Highlanders who came to North Carolina. In Scotland, such people lived in huts constructed either of sod or of stones, without windows or chimney. A hole in the roof at the center of the room provided some escape for the smoke and allowed a small amount of light to enter. In one end of the home the livestock spent the winter, with only a few bars separating this area from the living space. The more fortunate had a bedchamber adjoining the main room; most simply slept on the ground around the fires. Within the cabin could be found a table, one or two stools, a chain suspended from the ceiling and hanging from the chain an iron pot, a shelf, a chest or dresser, and a blanket and mattress, both filthy.[134] Homes for this class in North Carolina were constructed of better building material. Log homes with shingled roofs were cleaner, better able to withstand rain, and had chimneys. Most homes originally had earthen floors, but the ready supply of lumber made it possible later to lay wooden floors. Crude furniture could be more easily constructed in North Carolina, where wood was plentiful. Most settlers also had tables, stools, beds, and chests.[135] Although the migrant of the tenant class did not have many new possessions or luxuries in America, it is clear that he resided in a home that was superior to the Highland huts. One witness before a Loyalist Claims Court called the log house of John Macloud "furnished well." Macloud valued his log house and contents at £350 currency.[136] Further, the ready access to productive land and the bounty of nature provided a larger food supply for the tenant class that settled in America. In North Britain, however, tenants in the last half of the eighteenth century had little besides their staples of oatmeal and potatoes. Thomas Pennant was horrified to find Highland babies starving on the island of Cannay when he visited there in 1772.[137] The Highlander in North Carolina had prospects of further improving his lot, but the pressure of population and the inadequate food supply in Scotland gave the average tenant there less hope of bettering his living conditions. In summary, while migration did not greatly change the living conditions of the tacksmen, it did result in improved conditions for the tenants.

From the time of their arrival in North Carolina, the Highlanders took an active role in the political life of North Carolina. James Innes, one of the first to settle in the colony, had the most impressive record of public service. As early as 1734, he accepted the post of justice of the peace in New Hanover precinct.[138] At the outbreak of the War of Jenkins' Ear, North Carolina sent troops to join the British forces in the West Indies. In Admiral Vernon's disastrous assault on Cartagena, Innes, then a captain, commanded the North Carolina troops. He was among the few Carolinians to survive the battle.[139] After returning to North Carolina, he accepted a seat on the Council in 1750.[140] Innes was also known in other colonies as a military leader, and his role of greatest responsibility came during the French and Indian War. Governor Dinwiddie of Virginia appointed Innes, his close friend, as commander-in-chief of the expedition against the French and Indians in the Ohio Valley.[141] Innes, who was then a colonel, promptly made his will and proceeded to Virginia with a body of North Carolina troops. Upon hearing of the appointment, George Washington wrote Governor Dinwiddie that he was happy to serve under Innes, "an experienced officer and man of sense."[142] Because of orders from London, Innes was replaced as commander of all provincial troops four months later, but he continued as the commander of Fort Cumberland. James Innes served North Carolina both in life and in death, for his will allocated £100 for the establishment of a free school in the colony. Moreover, Innes remembered his friends and relatives in

Caithness. The will instructed the executors to purchase a bell for the parish of Cannesby in Caithness and to contribute £200 for the relief of the poor of that parish.[143]

Many other Highlanders took public positions. Only five months after the arrival of the group of 350 from Argyllshire, its leaders, Duncan Campbell, Dugald McNeil, "Coll" McAlister, and Neil McNeil, became justices of the peace.[144] In 1758 Hector McNeil claimed £10 as his salary as Cumberland County sheriff.[145] John Steward, another Highlander, succeeded McNeil.[146] Cumberland County representatives to the House of Assembly were usually Highlanders. Hector McNeil served in 1761, and Alexander McCallister (McAlister) joined him in the next year. In 1764, Farquard Campbell became a member of the House of Assembly and served until the outbreak of the Revolution.[147] Later Campbell was a delegate to several revolutionary conventions.[148]

James Hogg, the unhappy tacksman from Caithness who migrated to North Carolina because of the thievery and vandalism in the Highlands, came to play an unexpected role in the American political scene. For a short time, Hogg settled in Cross Creek and acted as the representative of his brother's firm of Hogg and Campbell.[149] Even before James Hogg had left Scotland, Robert Hogg had secured for him over 1000 acres of land near Hillsboro.[150] Since Hogg and Campbell maintained a branch in Hillsboro, James Hogg shortly moved to that town. Hogg and Campbell were successful merchants whose yearly profits amounted to some £1200. In 1778, when the partnership was dissolved, the company had assets of £18,330.[151] James Hogg, apparently because of his connections with his brother's firm and because of the income from his land holdings, had extra money to invest. At that same time, Judge Richard Henderson of

Hillsboro formed the Transylvania Company, which specu-
lated in land. James Hogg invested in the enterprise.
Henderson purchased the land between the Ohio, Cumberland, and Kentucky rivers from the Cherokee Indians and
sent settlers into the area under the leadership of Daniel
Boone in 1775.[152] Since crown regulations forbade settlement in this area, Henderson's newly organized government could not appeal to royal officials for recognition.
Judge Henderson decided to request a charter for the
Transylvania Colony from the revolutionary government.[153] James Hogg made the trip to Philadelphia as the
colony's representative. By this act, Hogg recognized the
Continental Congress and appears to have thrown in his lot
with the Patriots.[154] In spite of Hogg's best efforts, the
Congress denied his petition because the colony of Virginia claimed the land.[155] Hogg returned to North Carolina, where he served on the Hillsboro Committee of
Safety during the Revolution.[156] He was also one of the
first trustees of the University of North Carolina, which
opened its doors in 1795.[157]

It is noteworthy that the Cape Fear Highlanders
immediately accepted responsibilities in colonial government and produced several political leaders. They were
sure to become involved—one way or another—in the
revolutionary struggle that started in the 1770's.

CHAPTER VII

THE AMERICAN REVOLUTION

Awake on your hills, on your islands awake,
Brave sons of the mountain, the firth, and the lake!
'Tis the bugle—but not for the chase is the call;
'Tis the pibroch's shrill summons—but not to the hail.

'Tis the summons of heroes for conquest or death,
When the banners are blazing on mountain and heath,
They call to the dirk, the claymore, and the targe,
To the march and the muster, the line and the charge.
—from *Waverley*.[1]

To THOSE Highlanders who had hoped that by coming
to America they might escape the tears and travail of
repeated civil wars, the outbreak of the American Revolution must have come as a grim disappointment. Now for
the third time in the eighteenth century, the Highlanders
had to go through the agony of choosing sides, to accept
the strain and the waste of battle, and to face a bitter
defeat. Considering both their military experience and
their military reputation, it is understandable that they
were drawn into the revolutionary conflict in North Carolina. In view of their previous history, the remarkable development is that in this war they are found defending
"the bastards of Hanover." What can account for this
switch in allegiance? How was it possible to transform
chronic rebels into dogged Loyalists? It is the purpose

of this chapter to describe the events leading to the Battle of Moore's Creek Bridge and, using contemporary sources, to explain as fully as possible the reasons for the Loyalist stand of the North Carolina Highlanders.

The outbreak of the American Revolution cannot be explained by a single cause or single act. In the American Revolution, as in the bloody French Revolution which occurred a few years later, there were many incidents and many factors which precipitated the conflict. Probably more than anything else, it was the accumulation of numerous grievances during the period from 1763 to 1775 which finally led the colonists to arms. Few, if any, of the Americans plotted rebellion from Britain during this time. But as Englishmen they did protest what they considered to be denials of their rights. In colony after colony in the decade before the war, angry citizens were arguing heatedly, subscribing lengthy petitions, attending angry protest meetings, and threatening economic reprisals against the mother country. The colonists were reacting to crown policies such as the Proclamation Line of 1763, the Sugar Act of 1764, writs of assistance, the Stamp Act, the Townshend Acts, the cost of quartering troops, the Tea Act, and the Coercive Acts.

The North Carolina Highlanders, living as a relatively isolated inland community, were not involved and probably not much concerned with many of these issues. Colonial documents fail to shed much light on the attitudes of the Highlanders toward crown policies before 1771. There are, however, some indications of the feelings and actions of the people of Cumberland County in regard to two prewar issues—the Stamp Act and the uprising of the Regulators.

William Tryon, one of North Carolina's most capable and effective colonial governors, had just taken office in

1765 when the stamp conflict arose. A staunch defender of the crown's prerogative, Tryon was able to quell the Regulators, but he failed to enforce the sale of the hated stamps in the colony. Even before the passage of the Stamp Act, when the news reached North Carolina in October, 1764, that such a bill was contemplated, the Assembly expressed its conviction that no other body had the right to impose taxes upon the citizens of the colony.[2] After the Stamp Act became law, the residents of the lower Cape Fear area centering around Wilmington protested vigorously. They burned in effigy a supporter of the tax.[3] When two merchantmen without stamps on their port-clearance papers entered the mouth of the Cape Fear and were seized by British warships, several hundred people from Wilmington marched en masse to Brunswick to demand the release of the ships.[4] Much to Governor Tryon's chagrin, the British officers met with the leaders of the delegation and agreed to release the two ships. Tryon rightly believed that this concession would result only in further mob activity later, since it appeared to achieve its purpose.[5] Dr. William Houston, the royal official in charge of the sale of the stamps in the colony, was forced to resign his post by the people of Wilmington.[6] The courts of the colony ceased to function because people either refused to, or could not, purchase the necessary stamps for legal papers.[7] Finally, to the relief of everyone, Parliament repealed the Stamp Act.

The people of Cumberland County were concerned about the proposed stamp tax, and some of them openly opposed it. Unfortunately, we do not know to what degree the Highlanders were involved. In the fall of 1765, a group of the Cross Creek inhabitants gathered to burn in effigy Dr. Houston, the stamp officer, and a certain "M'Carter," who had murdered his wife.[8] Several months later a letter in the *North Carolina Gazette* signed by a man who identified himself only as a Cross Creek trader and settler called upon the citizens of North Carolina to open by force the mouth of the Cape Fear and to drive out the British warships.[9] For printing the letter, Andrew Stewart, a Highlander with the title of "His majesty's printer for this province," lost his commission.[10]

In the Regulation controversy, the Highlanders played a more active role. The dispute, which began with peaceful petitions by the Piedmont planters in 1765, ended in the Battle of Alamance in 1771.[11] The planters, underrepresented in the Assembly, lived in a region where money was scarce. The petitioners protested the illegal fees demanded by clerks and county registers of deeds and the illegal levying and collecting of taxes.[12] To secure the redress of their grievances, the Regulators stopped paying taxes, invaded the courts to halt the proceedings, and whipped court officials whom they captured.[13] After several attempts to appease them, Governor Tryon in 1771 determined to restore law and order in the Piedmont area. Calling up the militia, he organized two military groups to march into the Regulator territory.[14] In Cumberland County the Governor ordered Farquard Campbell and James Rutherford to raise 100 men. Campbell, the long-time political leader of the Highlanders, indicated there would be no difficulty in raising the men.[15] This would seem to show that the Cumberland people were not in sympathy with the Regulators. However, three years earlier, Judge Edmund Fanning had charged that the "principal men of Cumberland" were encouraging the Regulators.[16] On one occasion, it was reported in the Colonial Assembly that Regulators meeting at Cross Creek had decided to march on the Assembly.[17] In Anson County, where some of the Highlanders lived, there was much agitation by the Regulators; and in May, 1768, a mob there forced the court to disband.[18]   If the Highlanders were involved with the Regulators during the early years of the movement, and they may well have been, they made no attempt to stand with the Regulators in the crucial year of 1771.   One of the Governor's armed columns which marched from Wilmington to Salisbury passed through both Cumberland and Anson counties without any difficulty from Regulators there.   In fact, General Waddell increased his troops in Cumberland and Anson counties.[19]   Finally, on May 16, 1771, the Regulators and Governor Tryon's army met in Guilford County, and in the ensuing Battle of the Alamance, Tryon's militiamen defeated the underarmed and disorganized Regulators.[20]   Having successfully suppressed the rebels, Tryon immediately departed for New York to take his post as governor of that colony.[21]

Josiah Martin, the last royal governor of North Carolina, was the unfortunate man chosen to succeed Tryon. His hectic five years in the colony witnessed a constant deterioration of relations between the Governor and the Assembly.   During Tryon's term the Assembly had occasionally co-operated with the Governor; during Martin's term co-operation appeared to be a sign of weakness, and neither side would make concessions.   For that reason, little legislation was passed after 1771.   Martin's term began with hostility in the colony and ended with war.

In the years 1771 to 1775, several disputes created ill will between Governor and Assembly.   The first issue was the treatment of the defeated Regulators.   After visiting them, the new Governor became sympathetic to their plight and advocated an official pardon for the Regulators, but the Assembly, still dominated by men from the coastal region, refused.   By his sympathetic policy, the Governor

attached the Regulators to himself.[22]   A second issue was
the marking of the North Carolina–South Carolina line in
1772.   In his instructions from the Board of Trade, Governor Martin had been ordered to co-operate with South
Carolina in establishing the boundary.   The North Carolina Assembly, which felt that the line as determined in
London robbed the colony of part of its territory, refused
either to pay the surveying costs or to recognize it as a
valid line.[23]   A third issue related to the collection of a
tax designed to raise money for a sinking fund.   The
Assembly indicated that the tax had achieved its goal
and rescinded it.   When the Governor vetoed the bill,
the Assembly asked sheriffs in the colony not to collect
the tax.[24]   In this extralegal way, the representatives over-
rode the Governor's traditional role in the legislative
process.   The fourth conflict centered around a proposal
to create new courts in North Carolina.   A dispute arose
about the powers of the courts.   Both the Council and
the Governor insisted that the courts could not attach the
property of people in Europe without giving one year's
notice, but the Assembly would not agree.   As could be
anticipated, these conflicts produced hostility on both
sides.

Beginning in 1773, events outside the colony served to
widen the gap between Governor and Assembly.   Leaders
of the lower house by the latter part of 1773 despaired of
working with the Governor and were willing to make
bolder moves.   As a protest against the tax on tea, the
Assembly organized a Committee of Correspondence designed to share grievances with other colonies and to
co-ordinate actions.[25]   When the British government responded to the Boston Tea Party with the Intolerable
Acts, many North Carolinians were aroused.   The leading men of Wilmington met in July of 1774 to protest the

cruelties at Boston and the closing of the port. Among those signing the protest were Archibald Maclaine, a prominent merchant whose people had come from the island of Mull, and Robert Hogg, brother of James Hogg.[26] William Hooper, the signatory to the Declaration of Independence, reported in August, 1774, that the people of Wilmington had "very proper resentment for the injustice done."[27] Much to Governor Martin's dismay, the leaders of the Assembly called a revolutionary congress to meet late in August, 1774. This First Provincial Congress was widely attended. Among the delegates were Farquard Campbell and Thomas Rutherford from Cumberland County.[28] The delegates resolved to halt all commercial intercourse with Britain. They also named three representatives to the Continental Convention.[29] Revolutionary government in North Carolina was established by the fall of 1774. The Governor was powerless to stop it.

During the following months, groups of Patriots formed Committees of Safety to administer the non-importation agreement and to coordinate opposition to the Governor.[30] The Wilmington Committee published the names of individuals who refused to sign the non-importation agreement and forced them to appear before the Committee. By such actions and by threatening boycotts of merchants, they secured cooperation.[31] Even John Slingsby, a Cross Creek Loyalist who became a British officer during the Revolution, accepted the ban on importation. In December, 1774, Slingsby informed the Wilmington Committee that the brig *Diana* had just brought £1916 worth of goods for his store in Cross Creek and that he was delivering the goods to them to be disposed of as they wished.[32]

Events moved swiftly in North Carolina in April and May of 1775. Governor Martin called a meeting of the

Colonial Assembly at New Bern for April 4. The leaders of the Assembly summoned the Second Provincial Congress to meet at the same place on April 3, since many delegates to the Assembly were also delegates to the Congress.[33] When the leaders of the Assembly recessed that body to discuss the business of the Congress, Martin angrily prorogued the Assembly.[34] It was the last royal Assembly held in colonial North Carolina. Government was clearly in the hands of the revolutionary groups now, and the Governor was helpless. When news of the Battle of Lexington reached North Carolina early in May, the Committees of Safety began to make military preparations.[35] A meeting of concerned colonists gathered in Charlotte on May 31. They called for the election of colonial military officers who would act "independent of Great Britain."[36] The Governor realized he was not safe in New Bern. After his wife, "big with child," had successfully escaped New Bern, Governor Martin fled to the safety of a warship anchored in the mouth of the Cape Fear River.[37] There he remained for several years, subsisting, as one report has it, on biscuit and wild cabbage. When his slaves were able to get them, he added fish and oysters to his diet. Sir Henry Clinton visited Martin in 1776 and described him as being "literally half starved."[38]

From the safety of his floating command post aboard the *Cruizer* or the *Scorpion,* Governor Martin directed the counterrevolution. Even before his exile, the Governor had made plans for a military campaign in the colony. In a letter to General Gage dated March 16, 1775, Martin asked for "two or three stands of arms and some good ammunition" in order to halt the "insulting Gasconading" of the rebellious elements. He told Gage of offers of support from the Regulators and "a considerable body of

Highlanders."[39] Some action had to be taken, as Martin
well knew, to rescue the fast-sinking authority of the
crown. Janet Schaw, visiting in Wilmington at that time,
recognized the same need. After watching the intimida-
tion of loyal subjects who refused to sign a rebel "Test"
she wrote in June of 1775, "Oh Britannia what are you
doing, while your true obedient sons are thus insulted by
their unlawful brethren; are they also forgot by their
natural parents?"[40]

The Governor's plan for recovering the colony was revealed in greater detail in a series of letters to the Earl
of Dartmouth, Secretary of State for the Colonies.[41] Martin had formerly held the commission of lieutenant colonel,
but had sold it in 1769. He requested that he be allowed
to recruit a battalion of a thousand Highlanders in North
Carolina and that his old rank be restored. Martin's petition nominated his chief subordinate officers:

I would most humbly beg leave to recommend Mr. Allen
McDonald of Kingsborough to be Major, and Captain Alexd
McLeod of the Marines now on half pay to be first Captain
who besides being men of great worth, and good character,
have most extensive influence over the Highlanders here,
great part of which are of their own names and families,
and I should flatter myself that His Majesty would be gra-
ciously pleased to permit me to nominate some of the Sub-
alterns of such a Battalion, not for pecuniary consideration
but for encouragement to some active and deserving young
Highland Gentlemen who might be usefully employed in the
speedy raising of the proposed Battalion. Indeed I cannot
help observing My Lord, that there are three or four Gentlemen of consideration here, of the name of McDonald, and
a Lieutenant Alexd McLean late of the Regiment now on half
pay, whom I should be happy to see appointed Captains in
such a Battalion, being persuaded they would heartily promote
and do credit to His Majesty's Service.[42]

Martin's estimate of the Loyalist sentiments of the Regulators and Highlanders was accepted in Whitehall, but Dartmouth turned down the Governor's request for a commission.[43]   Martin, who had already sent an order to New York for "a good tent and markee, of the size of the Colonel's tent," complete with "mattress, bolster and pillows," was displeased that his request had been refused, but he continued planning a military campaign.[44]

Meanwhile, the Governor was sending messages to people of Loyalist sentiments in the western counties, encouraging them to stand by the King. Apologizing for his own unwillingness to risk the wrath of the Patriots, he advised James Cotton of Anson County, "You, and the other friends of Government, have only to stand your ground firmly, and unite against the seditious as they do against you, in firm assurance that you will be soon and effectually supported. I wait here to forward the purposes of the friends of Government, or I would have been among you. At the proper season you may depend I shall render myself among you, and in the mean time let nothing discourage you."[45]

During the last half of 1775, both the Governor and the Patriots worked to secure the greater number of adherents and particularly to influence the Highlanders and Regulators. On August 8, Governor Martin issued a lengthy proclamation denouncing the leaders and delegates of the forthcoming Hillsboro Provincial Congress. The manifesto was designed to intimidate those inclined to support the Congress.[46]   In New Bern, where the Governor formerly resided, the Committee of Safety issued a counterstatement ridiculing the Governor's enormous proclamation (six feet long and three feet wide) and branding it "a compound of falsehood and illiberal abuse" from the pen of "a contemptible scribbler."[47]   To prevent those Highlanders and Regulators who either visited or corresponded with the Governor from doing so any longer,[48] the Committee ruled that all communications with Governor Martin henceforth were to cease.[49] The Provincial Congress which met at Hillsboro in August, 1775, was uneasy about the political leanings of "the Gentlemen who have lately arrived from the highlands in Scotland" and appointed a committee to explain to them "the Nature of our Unhappy Controversy with Great Britain." Included in the twelve-man committee were the following members of the Provincial Congress: Alexander Maclaine, Alexander McAlister, Farquard Campbell, James Hepburn, and Alexander McKay.[50] To this same Hillsboro meeting, Governor Martin sent a request for safe-conduct for a horse and coach which he had abandoned in the colony, asking that his secretary be allowed to convey the vehicle to the home of Farquard Campbell in Cumberland County. The embarrassed Campbell immediately protested such an arrangement and said he would not keep the horse and coach. Congress absolved him of any suspicion.[51]

Late in 1775, General Gage dispatched two officers to North Carolina to organize the Highlanders into military units, Brigadier General Donald McDonald and Colonel Donald McLeod.[52] Since the Highlanders were largely unarmed, they could not be expected to carry on a military campaign without support.[53] It was therefore decided to march them to the mouth of the Cape Fear, where they could receive weapons and join forces with other units. Although the ministry was more desirous of retaking Charleston than of beginning a campaign in North Carolina, Alexander Schaw, a friend of Governor Martin, argued persuasively that victory could be more easily achieved in North Carolina. Then, with North Carolina retaken, the Loyalist elements in the South Carolina back country could be supplied with arms and Charleston would fall.[54]

In December the plan of action was revealed. General Howe, who had replaced Gage, would dispatch Sir Henry Clinton and 2000 troops to the mouth of the Cape Fear from Boston. Meanwhile, the fleet would convey Lord Cornwallis and seven regiments from Ireland to join Clinton. The Highlanders and Regulators would march to the sea to be armed by this force.

Governor Martin's own plans now became concrete. On January 3, 1776, he was informed of the arrangements and ordered to have the Highlanders at Brunswick not later than February 15.[55] Acting swiftly, he called for the assistance of all the King's loyal subjects in putting down the "most horrid and unnatural rebellion that has been excited therein by traitorous, wicked and designing men." This proclamation of January 10, 1776, called up-on the Regulator and Highlander leaders to raise the royal standard, organize the friends of the King, and march the army to Brunswick.[56] The die was cast.

The six-month period from July, 1775, to January, 1776, was a time of tension for the Highlanders of North Carolina. We know now that at the end of that half-year period of consideration a large number of the Highland Gaels did "repair to the royal banner." That lengthy period of indecision has a point of its own, however, and it is quite necessary to note that the Highlanders gave encouragement to the rebels at this time in many ways. The loyalty of the Highlanders to the King was by no means an immediate, automatic, or unanimous response. Like a maiden torn between the pleadings of two suitors, listening first to the proposal of one and then to the entreaties of the other, the Highlanders in this period of revolutionary courtship gave encouragement to both sides.

Since the Highlanders were so important to Governor
Martin's plans, he was frequently in touch with them dur-
ing this critical time. We know that in June, 1775, Captain Alexander McLeod of the Highlander settlement
traveled down to Wilmington to communicate with the
Governor.[57] There were several messengers who trans-
mitted information between Martin and Allan Mc-
Donald.[58] The Wilmington Committee of Safety became
suspicious about this exchange after capturing some of the
Governor's couriers and reading his mail. As early as
July, 1775, the Committee voiced its fear that Allan
McDonald and James Hepburn, a Cross Creek lawyer,
were raising troops for a Loyalist army.[59] In October the
Governor informed the Earl of Dartmouth that he had
communicated with Farquard Campbell in order to "sound
his disposition in case of matters coming to extremity
here."[60] It is little wonder that several Committees of
Safety adopted resolutions in the fall of 1775 branding
those people receiving letters from the Governor or visiting him as "enemies of the liberties of the people." They
were to be "dealt with accordingly."[61]

But the Patriots were also making a play for the hand
of the Highlanders. It has already been noted that in
August, 1775, the Provincial Congress sent a twelve-man
delegation, including five Highlanders, to confer with
"the gentlemen who have lately arrived from the highlands
in Scotland." The purpose of this committee was "to
advise and urge them to unite with the other Inhabitants
of America in defence of those rights which they derive
from God and the Constitution."[62] Joseph Hewes, one of
North Carolina's delegates to the Continental Congress in
Philadelphia, was similarly concerned. Upon his request,
four Presbyterian clergymen of Philadelphia wrote a letter
to fellow-Presbyterians in North Carolina defending the

right to revolt. The letter was then printed and circulated in the colony.[63] Probably under the prodding of Hewes, the Continental Congress on November 28, 1775, adopted a resolution which provided "that two ministers of the gospel be applied to, to go immediately amongst the regulators and highlanders of North-Carolina, for the purpose of informing them of the nature of the present dispute between Great-Britain and the colonies; that the gentlemen to be employed be allowed forty dollars for their services. . . ."[64] With the blessing of the Congress, Hewes then picked the Reverend Elihu Spencer and the Reverend Alexander McWhorter as his revolutionary missionaries.[65] A similar attempt to gain the confidence of the Highlanders was made in the circulation of a letter by a writer who urged the Highlanders to break publicly with the crown or declare neutrality in the struggle. The writer himself hid behind the assumed name "Scotus Americanus." Speaking of the revolutionary cause, he pleaded with his fellow Scots, "If we cannot be of service to the cause, let us not be of injury to it."[66]

Many of the Gaels were active in the new revolutionary organizations which appeared in 1774 and 1775. Outraged over the recent British firing on colonials at Lexington and Concord, a group of settlers from the Cross Creek area formed, in 1775, what was known as the Cumberland County Association. The document these settlers signed warned the British that "whenever our Continental or Provincial Councils shall decree it necessary, we will go forth and be ready to sacrifice our lives and fortunes to secure . . . freedom and safety."[67] Among the fifty-six signers were five men who were probably Highlanders: Thomas Rhea, Walter Murray, James Giles, William Gillespy, and James Gee. Although Cumberland County itself did not have a Committee of Safety, the records of the Wilmington Committee indicate that Farquard Campbell and Robert Cochran of Cumberland County were visiting members of that revolutionary tribunal.[68] Alexander Legate, a prominent Highlander, was a member of the Committee of Safety in Bladen County.[69]

The Provincial Congress of North Carolina was the chief policy-making body for the Patriots of the colony. It drafted and directed the plan of opposition to the crown. Certainly much of the credit for the success of the revolution in North Carolina should be assigned to this organization. It carried on a constant propaganda barrage, directed the Committees of Safety, enforced the boycott on English goods, and raised a revolutionary army. There were three conventions of the Provincial Congress before the Battle of Moore's Creek Bridge. Cumberland County was represented by Highlanders at each of the meetings. The delegates to the first convention held in August, 1774, and the second convention in April, 1775, were Thomas Rutherford and Farquard Campbell.[70] The first two meetings were at New Bern. When the Third Provincial Congress met at Hillsboro in August, 1775, a five-man delegation attended—Farquard Campbell, Thomas Rutherford, Alexander McKay, Alexander Mc-Alister, and David Smith.[71] These men were respected leaders in their community. Campbell had been a Cumberland County delegate to the Assembly for eleven years, from 1764 to 1775.[72] McAlister had been in the Assembly as early as 1762, and he had also served in 1773.[73] Thomas Rutherford was in the Assembly with Campbell in 1774-75.[74] This same convention made provisions for the defense of the colony by organizing groups of Minute Men in the several counties. The names of the officers of the Cumberland County Minute Men are significant. Those appointed were Thomas Rutherford, Colonel; Alexander

McAlister, Lieutenant Colonel; Duncan McNeil, First Major; Alexander McDonald, Second Major.[75]

In the fall of 1775, then, there was clearly a split in the leadership of the Highlanders. Allan McDonald and several other newly arrived Highlanders who were re- tired British officers advocated loyalty to the King. Mean- while, James Campbell, the long-time minister of the settlement,[76] and the veteran political leaders of the High- lander colony were playing open and active roles in the rebellion. Little wonder that Governor Martin wrote despairingly to the Earl of Dartmouth in October of 1775, "I have heard too My Lord with infinitely greater surprise and concern that the Scotch Highlanders on whom I had such firm reliance had declared themselves for neutrality, which I am informed is to be attributed to the influence of a certain Mr. Farquard Campbell an ignorant man who has been settled from his childhood in this County, is an old Member of the Assembly and has imbibed all the American popular principles and prejudices."[77]   A rec- ognition of the fact that the Highlanders were divided is important for an understanding of what happened at Cross Creek on February 12, 1776, when Brigadier General Donald McDonald called on the Highlanders to muster into the King's forces. Although Thomas Rutherford was a colonel in the Minute Men, he showed a remarkably im- partial spirit by accepting a similar commission in General McDonald's forces. With regard to the initial response to General McDonald's manifesto, Rutherford reported that "great numbers of His Majesty's liege subjects have failed to attend."[78]   The Highlanders did not rush pell- mell to defend the honor of George III. The decision was slow and painful.

A week after this first muster, however, General Mc- Donald was able to mass a much larger body of High-

landers, and by the end of the month those troops had
gone into battle for the royal cause. What forces in-
fluenced these Gaels to stand with the King? Can their
decision be explained? Since so many people were involved, motivation was sure to be complex and varied.
Contemporary documents do, however, give us clues to
at least four major reasons for the decision.

In the first place, the British in the eighteenth century
were remarkably successful in pacifying former enemies.
The two prime examples of this facility are their relations
with the French Canadians and with the Scottish Highlanders. In 1755, at the outset of the French and Indian
War, the British were so suspicious of the French settlers
of Nova Scotia that thousands of Cajuns were abruptly
scattered to other English colonies, thereby bringing great
hardship on the people and also creating the historical
background for Longfellow's "Evangeline." Only twenty
years later, the French Canadians were sufficiently loyal
to the British government that they refused all invitations
to join the American rebellion, even after France entered
the conflict on the American side. Not even the clever
appeals of America's best diplomat, French-speaking Ben
Franklin, could persuade them to attack the forces of
George III. According to Canadian historians, the Quebec
Act played a major role in pacifying the French Canadians.[79] By establishing the Catholic Church, the British
government secured the friendship and support of the
clergy. Given an important voice in government, the
seigniors, too, became loyal. For these reasons, General
Montgomery's invasion of Canada in 1775-76 did not
receive the hoped-for French support, and he failed to take
Canada. The Continental Congress, recalling the traditional French hatred for the British government, used

a variety of arguments in their letters to the inhabitants of Canada.

. . . it is our earnest desire to adopt them into our union, as a sister colony. . . .[80]

[We have expected that] our brave enemies would become our hearty friends.[81]

We are informed you have already been called upon to waste your lives in a contest with us. Should you, by complying in this instance, assent to your new establishment, and a war break out with France, your wealth and your sons might be sent to perish in expeditions against their islands in the West Indies.[82]

As our concern for your welfare entitles us to your friendship, we presume you will not, by doing us injury, reduce us to the disagreeable necessity of treating you as enemies.[83]

Neither the proffered hand of friendship, nor the threat of reprisal, nor lengthy arguments about the "rights of Englishmen"[84] moved the French to aid the American rebels. They were satisfied. British colonial policy toward the French Canadians had been successful in neutralizing a large number of former enemies.

Similarly, the British had effected a conciliation with the Scottish Highlanders during approximately the same period of time. In 1773, Samuel Johnson favored permitting the Highlanders to wear their colorful, distinctive garb again.[85] The Highlands had undergone many changes since the Forty-five. Woolen and linen mills now operated at several locations. New schools, employing only the English language, were to be found all over the Highlands. The 800 miles of road which had been built destroyed much of the provincialism and isolation of the Highlanders. The migration of many people to other parts of the British Isles or to America gave those who remained in the Highlands family ties outside their local area.[86] It was William Pitt who recognized that the Highlanders and the Highlands had so changed that there was no longer danger of revolution. Knowing their reputation as soldiers and needing troops during the Seven Years' War, Pitt decided to raise Highland regiments. They served Britain with distinction. He remarked after the war, "I sought only for merit and I found it in the mountains of the North; I there found a hardy race of men, able to do the country service, but labouring under a proscription: I called them forth to her aid and sent them forth to fight her battles. They did not disappoint my expectations, for their fidelity was equal to their valour."[87] A little over a decade later, when the American Revolution developed, London again called on the Highlanders for help. Samuel Johnson reported that the Highlanders responded immediately when their local leaders requested men for military duty.[88] When the war was over, the Lord Advocate, Henry Dundas, informed the House of Commons that no group of subjects in the empire had better demonstrated their loyalty than the Highlanders.[89] The remarkable change in the Highlanders' attitude is recorded in a poem entitled "On the Restoration of the Forfeited Estates, 1784":

> Ye northern chiefs, whose rage unbroke,
> Has still repelled the tyrant's shock;
> Who ne'er have bowed beneath her yoke
> With servile, base prostration;
> Let each now train his trusty band
> 'Gainst foreign foes alone to stand,
> With undivided heart and hand,
> For freedom, king, and nation.[90]

Historians in our own time who have been puzzled over the Loyalism of the Highlanders have failed to observe this shift of allegiance in the years following the Forty-five. The Americans, however, were fully aware of it at the time of the Revolution. In Virginia, Loyalists were referred to as "the Scotch party."[91] General Schuyler of New York despaired of securing the cooperation or aid of the Loyalist Highlanders in his colony. He added, "These people have been taught to consider us in politics in the same light that *Papists* consider *Protestants*."[92] In a letter to General Lee, John Page of Virginia wrote that it would disturb George III to know that "seven hundred and fifty of his favorite Highlanders" were captured.[93] John Witherspoon of Princeton, who gave dedicated support to the revolutionary cause, included in a sermon of May, 1776, an appeal to Scottish-born Americans to support the rebellion. He observed that so many Scottish people were faithful to the King that the word *Scotch* was becoming a term of reproach in America.[94] It was Witherspoon who persuaded the Continental Congress to remove the charge against the Scots which Jefferson had included in his first draft of the Declaration of Independence.[95] When a group of Highlanders were captured by the Americans during the war, they had the misfortune of being marched as prisoners from town to town. One of the Highlanders reported the experience: "On our journey no slaves were ever served as we were; through every village, town and hamlet that we passed, the women and children, and indeed some men among them, came out and loaded us with the most rascally epithets calling us 'rascally cut-throat dogs, Murtherers, blood hounds,' etc, etc. But what vexed me most was their continually slandering of our country [Scotland] on which they threw the most infamous invectives. . . ."[96]

We have already noted in chapter v that many of the North Carolina Highlanders came from Argyllshire. This was Campbell territory. For these Highlanders, it was part of their tradition to defend the House of Hanover.

During the Revolution, then, the Americans became painfully aware of the success of the British in turning their old French and Scottish enemies into neutrals or allies. In taking a Loyalist position in 1776, the Highlanders of North Carolina were not departing from the stand of Highlanders in other parts of the empire. They were only following the tide.

The fear of reprisal was probably a second factor motivating the Highlanders. Certainly Governor Martin, General McDonald, and Colonel Rutherford, all of whom made threatening statements, believed that fear of reprisal would work to the advantage of the crown. No group of people in the empire was any better acquainted with the painful aftermath of an unsuccessful revolution than the Highlanders. No doubt they read with concern the words of Governor Martin when he proclaimed that people who refused to stand with the monarch might well discover "their lives and properties to be forfeited."[97] A similar threat came from Brigadier General McDonald: "in case any person or persons shall offer the least violence to the families of such as will join the Royal standard, such person or persons, may depend that retaliation will be made; the horrors of such proceedings it is hoped will be avoided by all true Christians."[98] Colonel Thomas Rutherford made the threat more general when he posted this statement at Cross Creek: "This is, therefore, to command, enjoin, beseech and require all His Majesty's faithful subjects within the County of Cumberland to repair to the King's Royal Standard at Cross Creek, on or before the 16th present, in order to join the King's army; otherwise they must expect to fall under the melancholy consequences of a declared rebellion and expose themselves to the just resentment of an injured, though gracious Sovereign."[99]   Even those Highlanders who were too young to remember the Forty-five had heard many stories of the brutalities, atrocities, and destruction inflicted by the British Army under the Duke of Cumberland.

> And through the Highlands they were so rude,
> As leave them neither clothes nor food,
> They burnt their houses to conclude;
> 'Twas tit for tat.[100]

The North Carolina Highlanders were in a precarious position. If they sided with the King, there was the danger of reprisal from the Patriots. If they took up the rebel cause, they might be forced to re-experience the post-Culloden sufferings. As they made their decision, they probably remembered how difficult it was to overthrow Hanoverian rule and how painful it was to fail.

Governor Martin's land-grant policies must have been a third factor influencing some of the Highlanders when they were forced to make their choice. As has been noted earlier, the pressure of population and the changes in the agricultural system in the Highlands forced many people from the land. Thus the Highlanders' land hunger is understandable. The lengthy description of North Carolina by "Scotus Americanus" gave the views of a Highlander on the New World. For him, the most impressive characteristic of America was the abundance of good land.[101]   A large body of emigrants from Scotland came to North Carolina in 1775, as we have seen. The exiled Governor Martin, who was at that time aboard his floating executive mansion at the mouth of the Cape Fear, greeted a number of Highlander ships when they arrived.

Knowing that he had no power to prevent the Highlanders from seizing crown land for their settlement, he
decided to grant them land freely in return for an oath
declaring their "firm and unalterable loyalty and attachment to the King, and . . . their readiness to lay down
their lives in the support and defence of his Majesty's
Government."[102] The Board of Trade adopted a similar
policy in 1775 to encourage enlistments in the Royal
Regiment of Highland Emigrants. The following document was given to new recruits:

The bearer hereof, *Duncan McArthur,* having voluntarily engaged to serve His Majesty in the Royal Regiment of Highland Emigrants, (raised and established for the just and loyal
purpose of opposing, quelling, and suppressing the present
most unnatural, unprovolked and wanton rebellion,) con-
formable to the orders and directions of his Excellency the
Commander-in-chief, and agreeable to His Majesty's most
gracious intentions, signified by the Earl of Dartmouth,
(Secretary of State for America,) that such emigrants from
North-Britain, as well as other loyal subjects, that should en-
gage to serve in the before-mentioned corps, should be considered in the most favourable light; and after the conclusion
of the present unhappy civil war, (to which period only they
are obliged to serve,) be entitled to a proportion of two
hundred acres vacant (or forfeited) lands for every man or
head of a family, together with fifty acres more in addition
for every person the family may consist of; the whole to be
granted and patented without any expense to the said grantees.
And, moreover, to be free of any quit-rent to the Crown for
twenty years.[103]

This contract with Duncan McArthur was made in
Boston in December, 1775. Most members of the Royal
Regiment of Highland Emigrants were either from New
York or Nova Scotia. Although this writer has not dis-
covered copies of any such contracts made with North
Carolina Highlanders, it is possible that some North Caro-

linians made similar agreements with Brigadier General McDonald. We do know that Governor Martin was directed in April, 1775, to set aside a special area in North Carolina for such Highlander recruits.[104] We know also that the British government planned to organize the North Carolina Highlanders into the Second Battalion of the Royal Highland Emigrants when they reached the mouth of the Cape Fear.[105]

It has been observed that some Highlanders who received land took loyalty oaths. How binding were such oaths? Just as in our own day, not all who took oaths kept them. Probably the best example is Brigadier General McDonald. On the way to Cross Creek in 1775, he was detained in New Bern by the Patriots. They let him go when he took "a solemn oath" that he had neither military nor subversive intentions but was going to Cumberland County for social reasons.[106] That both sides continued to use oaths witnesses to the belief many people had in their efficacy.[107]

Regardless of the moot question of the effectiveness of oaths, the Highlanders did fear the loss of their land— some of it very recently acquired. They knew the crown had seized the land of the rebel clans after the Forty-five and, as of 1775, that the land still had not been returned to the original owners. Particularly did the possibility of the seizure of their land press upon those few Highlanders who still retained property in Scotland. In a letter to Cornelius Harnett, Dugall Campbell explained his unwillingness to join the Patriots. If he "took up arms for this country," said Campbell, "then my property will be immediately confiscated to the King."[108]

Some North Carolina Highlanders were retired officers on half pay, and their status as such was a fourth factor. Whether because of their past associations or their finan-

cial commitment, these men provided leadership for the
royal cause and were among the first to offer themselves
in the King's service.[109]   The leadership of Flora Mc-
Donald's husband, Allan, appears to have been of particular importance.   From Governor Martin's records, it
seems that McDonald was the earliest of the Highlanders
to offer his services.   Under the Governor's original plan,
Allan McDonald was to be second-in-command, with the
rank of major, and McDonald's son-in-law, Alexander
McLeod, was to be first-captain.   Governor Martin wrote
of McDonald and McLeod that "besides being men of
great worth, and good character, [they] have most extensive influence over the Highlanders here, great part
of which are of their own names and families."[110]   Since
Flora McDonald had been so greatly admired in the
Highlands, it was not unusual that many of the Gaels
looked to her husband for leadership in this crisis.   The
older leaders of the colony, as noted above, actively co-
operated with the revolutionary groups for a time, but
Allan McDonald never wavered in 1775 in his determina-
tion to stand with the King.   Governor Martin's letter
to the Earl of Dartmouth on November 12, 1775, describes
the jealousy the older leaders such as Farquard Campbell felt of Allan McDonald and Alexander McLeod.   The
older leaders were unhappy to observe the great influence
of the newcomers over the Highlander settlers.[111]   The
best proof of the part Flora's husband and son-in-law
played as leaders is to be seen in the fact that when
General Gage's two officers, Donald McDonald and
Donald McLeod, arrived in the Highlander settlement,
they found two companies of soldiers already organized
by Allan McDonald and Alexander McLeod.[112]

It is clear, then, that the decision of the Highlanders to
support one side or the other was not an automatic one.

Members of the group were active on both sides of the conflict. But a large body of Highlanders did come to the support of the King because of the considerations discussed above—the new feeling of friendship among the Highlanders for the House of Hanover, the fear of reprisal, the liberal land grants offered them, and the leadership of a number of retired British officers residing in the colony.

To the sound of the pibroch, the Highlanders mustered in Cross Creek in February, 1776. Only thirty-one years after their last great rebellion in the British Isles, they were the best friends George III had in the colony of North Carolina. In this moment of crisis it would have been appropriate for them to recite the verse so popular in the Highlands at that time:

> Haste Donald, Duncan, Dugald, Hugh!
> Haste, take your sword and spier!
> We'll gar these traytors rue the hour
> That e'er they ventured here.[113]

The Governor expected approximately 3000 Regulators to rise and a like number of Highlanders.[114] Among the Regulators the response was disappointing. Immediately after the Governor's proclamation had been issued, there was renewed Loyalist zeal in the Regulator counties.[115] But the Regulators did not flock to join the royal troops. One group of 500 gathered but when they began marching to Cross Creek, the sight of a company of Whigs dispersed them.[116] The total number of Regulators who fought at the side of the Highlanders in the royal cause in 1776 was under 200.[117] Why did the Regulators fall so short of the Governor's expectations? Some expressed dissatisfaction that most of the leaders were Highlanders.[118] Many had no weapons, since their guns had been seized in 1771. Moreover, they had felt the pain of losing in war, and they did not desire to take such a risk again.[119]

Among the Highlanders there was greater response, although again the numbers raised did not coincide with the Governor's estimate. During the first month of 1776, several Highlanders experienced a remarkable change in attitude. It was Thomas Rutherford, delegate to all the Provincial Congresses and head of the Cumberland County Minute Men, who issued the call for all "Lovers of Order and Good Government" to muster under the King's standard at Cross Creek on February 12, 1776. When only a few reported, Rutherford published another manifesto "to command, enjoin, beseech and require all His Majesty's faithful subjects . . . to repair to the King's Royal Standard at Cross Creek."[120] Alexander Legate, a member of the Committee of Safety of Bladen County, appeared at the muster and received a commission as captain.[121] One of the delegation sent by the Hillsboro Congress to speak to the Highlanders in the fall of 1775 was Alexander McKay; but when the royal standard was raised at Cross Creek, he joined the King's army.[122] Farquard Campbell, in January and February of 1776, sought to appear as a friend of both sides.[123] The ranks of the Patriot Highlanders thinned. Of the five Cumberland County delegates to the Hillsboro Congress, only two remained faithful to the American cause—David Smith and Alexander McAlister.[124]

Thomas Rutherford's calls supplemented the earlier proclamation of Brigadier General Donald McDonald, who on February 4, 1776, had asked all loyal subjects to join his army. At that time, McDonald had assured Loyalist men that their families and property would be protected and that any supplies or equipment seized by the army would be paid for.[125]   In spite of these promises, a total of only 1500 men joined the Loyalist forces. Thirteen hundred of them were Highlanders.[126]   Because of faulty intelligence reports, the Governor originally was led to believe that 7000 men had joined McDonald's forces.   Later he received reports that the group was made up of 3500 men.   Only after the Battle of Moore's Creek Bridge did he learn of the actual size of the Loyalist army.[127]

The Patriots soon were aware of the impending Loyalist march to the mouth of the Cape Fear.   The Committee of Safety in New Bern made plans at its meeting of February 10 to oppose the Highlanders.   Colonel Richard Caswell received an order from the Committee to mobilize his Minute Men for action.[128]   The people of Wilmington also exhibited concern over the Loyalist march to the sea, since Wilmington was on the route the army would take.   There was an added danger for Wilmington; British naval vessels might sail up the Cape Fear and bombard the city.   As a matter of fact, it was only the fortifications constructed around the city, together with rifle fire from both sides of the Cape Fear, that later did discourage a British warship from attacking the city.   To meet the Highlanders, two units of militia and Minute Men marched north from Wilmington.[129] Colonel James Moore, who commanded the Patriot troops, by forced march up the western side of the Cape Fear reached Rockfish Creek, blocking McDonald's path downstream.[130]

At this time the dual role of Farquard Campbell became evident.   Campbell visited the military encampments of both the Highlanders and the Patriots, giving each information about the other.[131]   Campbell informed Brigadier General McDonald that Moore expected reinforcements shortly. Since the King's forces would then be outnumbered, Campbell advised McDonald to avoid a battle. In the light of this information, the British general realized that his primary aim ought to be to lead his soldiers to the mouth of the Cape Fear and there to rendezvous with the forces from Boston under Sir Henry Clinton and seven regiments from the British Isles under the command of Lord Charles Cornwallis. McDonald feared that open battle would bring defeat, since his men were untrained and only half had firearms.[132] He accepted Farquard Campbell's advice, crossed the Cape Fear at Campbellton to evade Colonel Moore, and descended the east bank of the river.[133]

After evading Moore's army, the Loyalists marched steadily downstream until they encountered the Patriot forces drawn up at Moore's Creek Bridge, eighteen miles above Wilmington. Colonels Richard Caswell and Alexander Lillington had fortified an elevation overlooking the bridge that the Loyalists had to cross. To make that crossing more difficult, the floor boards of the bridge had been removed and the sleepers greased.[134]

Unfortunately for the Highlanders, Brigadier General McDonald, a conservative and capable officer, became ill and the command fell to Colonel Donald McLeod.[135] McLeod secured the approval of the other younger officers for an attack the following morning, indicating that he would lead the assault personally. The results of his leadership were disastrous for the Highlanders.[136] From concealed positions the Patriots fixed their rifle and artillery fire on the bridge as the Highlanders attempted to follow their leaders across the slippery beams. After the Patriots' first volley had swept the bridge clean, the Highlanders on the bank panicked and fled from the scene.[137] About 50 Highlanders were killed and 880 were cap-

tured. In sharp contrast, the Patriots lost only 2 men.[138]
The attempt of the Highlanders to come to the aid of
Governor Martin and the royal cause failed.

Defeat is always a bitter experience. The Highlanders
learned this after the Battle of Culloden; they redis-
covered it after the Battle of Moore's Creek Bridge. In
North Carolina, the aftermath of battle was not so bloody
as it had been in Scotland; still, it was a trying time. The
Highlanders who were captured were thrown into the
common jails of the colony.[139] As a consequence of their
imprisonment, the prisoners' families were left alone and,
often, unprotected. In the months after the battle, groups
of Whigs raided, pillaged, and burned Tory farms, caus-
ing much needless suffering.[140] Though most of the
Loyalist soldiers were captured, a few successfully concealed themselves in the woods after the battle. Since
the Whigs had captured General McDonald's muster lists,
these Loyalist soldiers could not return home. Instead,
they attempted to hike overland to join British units elsewhere.[141] Although the Committees of Safety forced
some Highlanders to leave North Carolina in 1776, the
Provincial Congress did not officially authorize such
policies until the next year. In April, 1777, the Provincial
Congress passed a law legalizing the banishment of non-
juring Loyalists and the confiscation of the property of
those who refused to take an oath of fealty to the Revolutionary government.[142] This legislation provoked a new
migration.

There are no reliable estimates of the numbers of
Loyalist Highlanders who left the state or of the size of
the group which remained in North Carolina. Robert O.
DeMond has made an extensive study of the Land Con-
fiscation Records, the Loyalist Claims, and the Pension
Rolls, but he does not attempt to estimate the number of

Highlanders who fled. We must rely upon the observations of contemporaries who observed the exodus. One concerned Whig declared that two-thirds of the people in Cumberland County were preparing to leave in the summer of 1777. This may have been a high estimate, but others at the same time wrote of the "great numbers" departing and described them as people of considerable wealth.[143] Where did the Loyalists go? A few moved south to Florida and the West Indies. Most went by ship to New York and then on to the British Isles or to Canada, where many settled in Nova Scotia.

In spite of retaliatory laws, confiscations, and pillaging, many Highlanders remained in the upper Cape Fear region, as the census returns of 1790 witness. After the Battle of Moore's Creek Bridge, however, Governor Martin realized it was impossible for him to exercise authority in North Carolina. His plan had failed. He abandoned his post at the mouth of the Cape Fear River.[144] When the British army finally did arrive—three months late—there was no chance of a successful campaign in North Carolina, so the troops of George III moved down the coast to Charleston.[145] Later, in 1781, Lord Cornwallis did lead a British army into North Carolina. He expected the Cape Fear Highlanders to flock into his army, but they were cold to his pleas. Many of the remaining Highlanders may have been Loyalists at heart, but they were unwilling to take up arms again.[146]

Although the eighteenth-century Highlanders were not always consistent in their attitude toward the House of Hanover, they were remarkably consistent in choosing the losing side in civil wars. In three separate conflicts they took up arms. In each war they were defeated. After each defeat they suffered from retributive legislation. Those who fled from North Carolina in the 1770's might well have recited the same verse sung by their ancestors a generation earlier:

Now forced from my home and my dark halls away,
The son of the strangers has made them a prey;
My family and friends to extremity driven,
Contending for life both with earth and with
    heaven![147]

APPENDIX

NAMES PLACED IN THREE CATEGORIES
FOR USE IN ANALYZING LAND GRANTS AND LAND
PURCHASES

Highlanders

Bain, William
Black, Donald
Buea, Archibald
Buea, Duncan
Buea, Malcom
Buea, Mary
Buea, Neill
Bug, Archibald
Cameron, Allan
Campbell, Archibald
Campbell, Donald
Campbell, Duncan
Campbell, Farquard
Campbell, John
Campbell, William
Campley, Archibald
Carmichael, Archibald
Carmichael, Dugald
Carmichael, Evan
Clark, Alexander
Clark, Gilbert
Clark, John
Clark, Neill
Colquhon, Archibald
Darach, Jenny
Douglass, Archibald
Duncan, James
Earl, Ronald
Ferguson, John
Galbreath, Angus
Gilchrist, John
Gordon, William

Grant, George
Gun, Donald
Matheson, Hugh
McAlister, James
McAlister, Coll
McAllum, Duncan
McArthur, Peter
McBeath, John
McBraine, Murdock
McCallum, Duncan
McCraine, Hugh
McCole, Donald
McCole, Dugald
McCole, Duncan
McCole, John
McDonald, Donald
McDonald, Hector
McDonald, William
McDougald, Alexander
McDougald, Angus
McDougald, Donald
McDougald, Dougald
McDougald, James
McDougald, John
McDougald, Malcom
McDougald, Peggy
McFarlane, Donald
McFerson, John
McGill, Archibald
McInish, Malcom
McIntyre, Donald
McIntyre, Duncan

McIntyre, Gilbert
McIntyre, John
McKay, Angus
McKay, Donald
McKay, George
McKay, James
McKay, William
McLachlan, James
McLaren, Lachlan
McLean, Donald
McLean, Duncan
McLean, John
McLean, Nanny
McLean, Peter
McLeod, Aeneas
McLeod, Alexander
McLeod, William
McMillan, Archibald
McMillan, Daniel
McMillan, Iver
McMullan, Malcom
McMurchie, Archibald
McMurchie, Patrick
McNabb, John
McNichol, Angus
McNichol, Donald
McNichol, John
McNichol, Robert
McNeill, Allan
McNeil, Daniel
McNeil, Hector
McNeil, Neil

McPherson, Malcom
McRay, William
McRob, Duncan
McVey, Dougald
McVicar, John
Monro, Hugo
Monro, William
Morison, Patrick

Pattison, Gilbert
Ross, John
Ross, Patrick
Sinclair, Alexander
Sinclair, Duncan
Sinclair, James
Sinclair, John
Sinclair, Peggy

Smith, Malcom
Stewart, Alexander
Stewart, Allan
Stewart, Archibald
Stewart, Dugald
Stewart, Kenneth
Stewart, Patrick
Sutherland, William

Probably Highlanders

Individuals bearing family names appearing in category one, "Highlanders," but possessing different Christian names, are considered to belong in this category. Added to the family names which appear in category one are the following new names:

Beard
Blue
Colbreath
Forbes
Frazier
Gray
MacNair
MacFatters
McAlpine
McCranie

McFee
McKisack
McLeran
McLairin
McLaughlan
Menzies
Munn
Ray
Rea
Urkquard

Possibly Highlanders

Family names that may be either Highland or Lowland names are placed in this category.

Baker
Best
Blake
Brice
Brown
Curry
Dunn
Gill

Graham
Legg
Little
Lyon
McAckeran
McAlexander
McAller
McBride

McCeithen
McClendon
McCleron
McConkey
McCoulskey
McCoy
McCracken
McCullerman
McCulloh
McDade
McDaniel
McDuffie
McEachern
McFaile
McFall
McFarling
McGathy

McGaw
McGoogin
McKee
McKeithen
McKeller
McKettron
McKinney
McLallen
McLoud
McNatt
McRaw
McReid
McSwine
McTagart
McWilkin
Patterson
Shaw
Strahan

For an explanation of the way in which names in this Appendix are organized, see pages 90-92.

NOTES

CHAPTER I

1. *Ancient Ballads and Songs of the North of Scotland,* ed., Peter Buchan (Edinburgh: W. and D. Laring, 1828), II, 148.

2. Samuel Johnson, *Journey to the Western Islands of Scotland* (Oxford: Oxford University Press, 1924), p. 87.

3. Thomas J. Wertenbaker, "Early Scotch Contributions to the United States," *Glasgow University Publications,* No. 64 (1945), pp. 9-10.

4. Charles W. Dunn presents a description of the ethnic background of the Highlanders in his *Highland Settler: A Portrait of the Scottish Gael in Nova Scotia* (Toronto: University of Toronto Press, 1953), pp. 1-7. For a map of the Highlands, see p. 5. Shire lines and place names are taken from the map on p. vii of Thomas Pennant's *A Tour of Scotland* (London: Benjamin White, 1790), I, and the map facing the title page of Sir John Sinclair's *General Report of the Agricultural State and Political Circumstances of Scotland* (Edinburgh: A. Constable and Co., 1814), I.

5. George P. Insh, *The Scottish Jacobite Movement: A Study in Economic and Social Forces* (Edinburgh: Moray Press, 1952), p. 126; George M. Trevelyan, *English Social History* (London: Longmans, Green & Co., 1942), pp. 446-47.

6. Edward Burt, *Letters from a Gentleman in the North of Scotland to His Friend in London,* ed. R. Jamieson (London: Ogle, Duncan & Co., 1954), II, 247.

7. *Ibid.,* pp. 145-48, 152, 163.

8. The record book of William Mackintosh, a Highland tacksman, provides much information about the living standards in Inverness-shire in the last half of the eighteenth century. Isabel F. Grant's *Everyday Life on an Old Highland Farm, 1769-1782* (London: Longmans, Green and Co., 1924) reprints this valuable record book with comments. For evidence of privation and starvation, see p. 61. An excellent essay on the topic is Margaret I. Adam's "Eighteenth Century Landlords and the Poverty Problem," *Scottish Historical Review,* XIX (April, 1922), 162.

9. Burt, *Letters,* III, 64, 99, 130-31.

10. *Ibid.,* p. 59.

11. Robert Ergang, *Europe from the Renaissance to Waterloo* (Boston: D. C. Heath & Co., 1939), p. 381.

12. R. L. Mackie, *Scotland* (London: George G. Harrap and Co., 1916), pp. 354-55.

13. Ergang, *Europe*, pp. 384-85, 388-400, 417-19.

14. Mackie, *Scotland*, pp. 376-77, 400-1, 406, 448-49.

15. Ergang, *Europe*, p. 398.

16. Mackie, *Scotland*, pp. 448-49, Ergang, *Europe*, pp. 420-26.

17. Robert S. Rait, *The Making of Scotland* (London: A. and C. Black, Ltd., 1929), pp. 284-85, 288-93.

18. *The Cambridge Modern History*, VI, 90-91; Mackie, *Scotland*, pp. 475-77; P. Hume Brown, *History of Scotland* (Cambridge, England: University Press, 1909), III, 163-66, 243, 269, 277, 281-82.

19. Mackie, *Scotland*, pp. 476-81.

20. Brown, *History of Scotland*, III, 185.

21. *The Cambridge Modern History*, VI, 102-3.

22. *Ibid.*, p. 97.

23. Brown, *History of Scotland*, III, 270-77.

24. Mackie, *Scotland*, p. 484.

25. Brown, *History of Scotland*, III, 276.

26. *Ibid.*, p. 288.

27. *Ibid.*, p. 282.

28. *Ibid.*, p. 311.

29. Mackie, *Scotland*, pp. 486-88; Brown, *History of Scotland*, III, 286-99.

30. *The Cambridge Modern History*, VI, 113.

31. Mackie, *Scotland*, p. 488.

32. Brown, *History of Scotland*, III, 305.

33. *Ibid.*, pp. 302-7; Mackie, *Scotland*, p. 489.

34. Brown, *History of Scotland*, III, 307-24; Mackie, *Scotland*, pp. 489-92.

35. Llewellyn Eardley-Simpson, *Derby and the Forty-five* (London: Philip Allan, 1933), p. 21.

36. *The Cambridge Modern History*, VI, 112, 116-17; Mackie, *Scotland*, p. 493.

37. Eardley-Simpson, *Derby and the Forty-five*, p. 21.

38. *Culloden Papers*, ed. Duncan Forbes (London: T. Cadell & W. Davies, 1815), p. 289.

39. *Journals of the House of Commons*, XXV (August 8, 1746), 186.

40. *Scots Magazine* (Edinburgh), VIII (August 8, 1746), 371.

41. *Journals of the House of Commons*, XXV (June 12, 1747), 404.

42. *Forfeited Estates Papers*, ed. A. H. Millar (Edinburgh: University Press, 1909), pp. 342-43; *Parliamentary History of England*, ed. Thomas C. Hansard (London: Thomas C. Hansard, 1813), XIV, 1235.

43. Rait, *The Making of Scotland*, pp. 277-80; *The Cambridge Modern History*, VI, 117; Brown, *History of Scotland*, III, 327-28.

44. *Jacobite Minstrelsy* . . . (Glasgow: Printed for Richard Griffin & Co., 1829), pp. 210-11.

45. *Jacobite Songs and Ballads*, ed. G. S. Macquoid (London: Walter Scott Publishing Co., n.d.), pp. 146-47.

46. "Letters from the Duke of Newcastle to the Lord Justice Clerk," *Prisoners of the '45,* eds. Sir Bruce G. Seton and Jean G. Arnot (Edinburgh: University Press, 1928), I, 221; *Scots Magazine,* VIII (August, 1746), 364-65.

CHAPTER II

1. *The Jacobite Relics of Scotland* collected and illustrated by James Hogg (Paisley: Alexander Gardner, 1874), p. 186.

2. Francois-Xavier Martin, *The History of North Carolina from the Earliest Period* (New Orleans: A. T. Penneman, 1829), p. 48.

3. William H. Foote, *Sketches of North Carolina* (New York: Robert Carter, 1846), pp. 129-30.

4. Eli Washington Caruthers, *Revolutionary Incidents: And Sketches of Character Chiefly in the Old North State* (Philadelphia: Hayes and Zell, 1854), p. 42.

5. Richard Webster, *A History of the Presbyterian Church in America* (Philadelphia: Joseph M. Wilson, 1857), pp. 63, 531.

6. James G. Craighead, *Scotch and Irish Seeds in American Soil* (Philadelphia: Presbyterian Board of Publications, 1878), p. 268. Craighead does not indicate his sources, but his division of the migrants into "forced" and "voluntary" suggests that he may have used Martin.

7. John P. MacLean, *An Historical Account of the Settlements of Scotch Highlanders in America Prior to the Peace of 1783* (Cleveland: Helman-Taylor Company, 1900), p. 104. Although MacLean and Charles A. Hanna, whose quotation appears below, do not acknowledge the source of their information, both follow Foote closely—sometimes word for word.

8. Charles A. Hanna, *The Scotch-Irish* (New York: G. P. Putnam's Sons, 1902), II, 34.

9. Enoch W. Sikes, "North Carolina as a Royal Province, 1729-1776," *The South in the Building of the Nation* (Southern Historical Publication Society), I, 445; Herbert L. Osgood, *The American Colonies in the Eighteenth Century* (New York: Columbia University Press, 1924), II, 522.

10. Robert D. W. Connor, *The History of North Carolina* (Chicago: Lewis Publishing Co., 1919), I, 156.

11. Samuel A'Court Ashe, *History of North Carolina* (Greensboro, N. C.: Charles L. Van Noppen, 1925), I, 266.

12. *Some Eighteenth Century Tracts Concerning North Carolina,* ed. William K. Boyd (Raleigh, N. C.: Edwards and Broughton Co., 1927), p. 491.

13. John H. Finley, *The Coming of the Scot* (New York: Scribner's, 1940), p. 86.

14. Hugh T. Lefler and Albert R. Newsome, *North Carolina: The History of a Southern State* (Chapel Hill: University of North Carolina Press, 1954), p. 73.

15. Thomas J. Wertenbaker, "Early Scotch Contributions to the United States," *Glasgow University Publications,* No. 64 (1945), pp. 8-9.

16. For an excellent discussion of this as applied to all the British colonies, see Ian C. C. Graham, *Colonists from Scotland: Emigration to North America, 1707-1784* (Ithaca, N. Y.: Cornell University Press, 1956), pp. 43-46. He believes the forced exile of Highlanders has been overemphasized in colonial history.

17. *Colonial Records of North Carolina,* ed. William L. Saunders (Raleigh: State Printer, 1886-90), IV, 956.

18. Abbot E. Smith, *Colonists in Bondage: White Servitude and Convict Labor in America, 1607-1776* (Chapel Hill: University of North Carolina Press, 1947), pp. 200-2.

19. *Colonial Records of North Carolina,* IV, 918.

20. *Ibid.,* pp. 925-45.

21. *Prisoners of the '45,* eds. Sir Bruce G. Seton and Jean G. Arnot (Edinburgh: University Press, 1928), I, 26. Seton and Arnot reached the above numbers by comparing Jail Rolls, State Papers (Domestic and Scottish), Patent Rolls, Treasury Records, and Admiralty and War Office Papers. Using Treasury Records, Abbot Smith computes that only 610 were actually transported. Abbot E. Smith, *Colonists in Bondage: White Servitude and Convict Labor in America, 1607-1776* (Chapel Hill: University of North Carolina Press, 1947), p. 201.

22. *Prisoners of the '45,* I, 26.

23. *Journals of the House of Commons,* XXV (May 29, 1747), 398.

24. For a humorous account of the imprisonment, transportation, and sale of a Highland soldier as an indentured servant in Maryland, see "Memorial of Alexander Stewart," *The Lyon in Mourning,* ed. Bishop Robert Forbes (Edinburgh: University Press, 1896), II, 231-47.

25. *Ibid.,* p. 240, and III, 22-23; Smith, *Colonists in Bondage,* pp. 201-2.

26. *Prisoners of the '45,* I, 27.

27. *Ibid.,* I, 40.

28. *Scots Magazine,* XVIII (May, 1748), 245.

29. *Gentleman's Magazine,* XVI (May, 1746), 261.

30. *Culloden Papers,* ed. Duncan Forbes (London: T. Cadell & W. Davies, 1815), p. 285.

31. *Prisoners of the '45,* I, 5.

32. *Parliamentary History of England,* ed. Thomas C. Hansard (London: Thomas C. Hansard, 1813), XIV, 1-57, 269-316; XIII, 1402-26.

33. *The Lyon in Mourning,* I, xiv.

34. North Carolina land grants are recorded in the office of the Secretary of State in Raleigh. For an explanation of the technique used in securing the land-grant statistics, see chapter v.

35. *Colonial Records of North Carolina,* IV, 490.

36. In the land grant list for 1746, Neal McNeal, Alexander Clark, and Hector McNeal are listed as having received grants before 1745.

37. In the land grant list for 1749, Daniel McNeal and Alexander McAlister are listed as having received grants before 1745.

CHAPTER III

1. *The Jacobite Relics of Scotland,* collected and illustrated by James Hogg (Paisley: Alexander Gardner, 1874), pp. 185-86.

2. *Culloden Papers,* ed. Duncan Forbes (London: T. Cadell & W. Davies, 1815), p. 299.

3. Samuel Johnson, *Journey to the Western Islands of Scotland* (Oxford: Oxford University Press, 1924), pp. 78-80; *Culloden Papers,* p. 298; Isabel F. Grant, *Everyday Life on an Old Highland Farm, 1769-1782* (London: Longmans, Green & Co., 1924), p. vi.

4. Sir John Sinclair, *General Report of the Agricultural State and Political Circumstances of Scotland* (Edinburgh: A. Constable and Co., 1814), II, 393-97, 402; Margaret I. Adam, "The Highland Emigration of 1770," *Scottish Historical Review,* XVI (July, 1919), 288.

5. Johnson, *Journey,* p. 78.

6. [Janet Schaw], *Journal of a Lady of Quality . . .,* eds. Evangeline W. Andrews and Charles McLean Andrews (New Haven: Yale University Press, 1921), p. 37.

7. Thomas Pennant, *A Tour in Scotland and Voyage to the Hebrides* (Chester, England: John Monk, 1774-76), II, 201.

8. James Boswell, "The Journal of a Tour to the Hebrides with Samuel Johnson," in Samuel Johnson, *Journey to the Western Islands of Scotland,* p. 246.

9. Pennant, *A Tour in Scotland,* II, 229.

10. Grant, *Everyday Life on an Old Highland Farm,* p. 79.

11. Boswell, "Journal of a Tour to the Hebrides," p. 263.

12. Pennant, *A Tour in Scotland,* II, 201; The Earl of Selkirk, *Observations on the Present State of the Highlands of Scotland* (Edinburgh: A. Constable & Co., 1806), p. 42.

13. Grant, *Everyday Life on an Old Highland Farm,* pp. 114-15, 40.

14. *Forfeited Estates Papers,* ed. A. H. Millar (Edinburgh: University Press, 1909), p. 207.

15. Johnson, *Journey,* p. 85.

16. *Edinburgh Advertiser,* XXIII (January 20, 1775), 49.

17. Sinclair, *General Report,* II, 397. For evidence of the character of services demanded see the complaints of emigrants as recorded in "Records of Emigrants from England and Scotland to North Carolina," *North Carolina Historical Review,* XI (April, 1934), 131-33.

18. *Scots Magazine,* XXXIV (Appendix, 1772), 698; a good analysis of this shift in class structure is to be found in Margaret I. Adam's "The Highland Emigration of 1770," *Scottish Historical Review,* XVI (July, 1919), 290.

19. *Forfeited Estates Papers,* pp. 77, 217; Pennant, *A Tour in Scotland,* II, 11; III, 36; Grant, *Everyday Life on an Old Highland Farm,* pp. 44-45, 48; Sinclair, *General Report,* II, 399-400, 408.

20. *Ibid.,* pp. 393, 402.

21. *Forfeited Estates Papers,* pp. 116, 140; Edward Burt, *Letters from a Gentleman in the North of Scotland to His Friend in London,* ed.

R. Jamison (London: Ogle, Duncan & Co., 1754), II, 134; Grant, *Everyday Life on an Old Highland Farm*, p. 59.

22. Burt, *Letters*, II, 132.

23. Grant, *Everyday Life on an Old Highland Farm*, p. 61.

24. "Letter from Flora McDonald to Mr. John MacKensie," August 12, 1772, *ap.* John A. Oates, *The Story of Fayetteville and the Upper Cape Fear* (Fayetteville, N. C.: Privately printed, 1950), p. 787.

25. Burt, *Letters*, II, 132.

26. Pennant, *A Tour in Scotland*, III, 265, 281, 402.

27. *Scots Magazine*, XXXIV (July, 1772), 395.

28. *Ibid.*, XXXVII (October, 1775), 536.

29. Charles W. Dunn, *Highland Settler: A Portrait of the Scottish Gael in Nova Scotia* (Toronto: University of Toronto Press, 1953), p. 12.

30. "Records of Emigrants from England and Scotland to North Carolina, 1774-1775," *North Carolina Historical Review*, XI (January and April, 1934), 48-54, 129-43.

31. *Scots Magazine*, XXV (October, 1773), 557.

32. *Ibid.*, XXXIV (Appendix, 1772), 699.

33. *Ibid.*, XXXIII (September, 1771), 500; XXXVII (December, 1775), 690.

34. Pennant, *A Tour in Scotland*, I, 228.

35. *The Lyon in Mourning*, ed. Bishop Robert Forbes (Edinburgh: University Press, 1896), III, 259.

36. *Scots Magazine*, XXXIV (July, 1772), 395.

37. "Records of Emigrants from England and Scotland to North Carolina, 1774-1775," *North Carolina Historical Review*, XI (April, 1934), 134.

38. Selkirk, *Observations*, chapter IV, especially pp. 44-45, 48-49; Sinclair, *General Report*, II, 398-99; *Forfeited Estates Papers*, p. 122.

39. "Records of Emigrants from England and Scotland to North Carolina, 1774-1775," *North Carolina Historical Review*, XI (April, 1934), 132-37.

40. *Ibid.*, pp. 138-42.

41. Pennant, *A Tour in Scotland*, II, 355-56.

42. "Records of Emigrants from England and Scotland to North Carolina, 1774-1775," *North Carolina Historical Review*, XI (April, 1934), 138-42.

43. Selkirk, *Observations*, p. xxxv.

44. *Some Eighteenth Century Tracts Concerning North Carolina*, ed. William K. Boyd (Raleigh, N. C.: Edwards and Broughton Co., 1927), p. 421.

45. *Ibid.*, p. 422.

46. *Ibid.*, p. 423.

47. *Ibid.*, p. 423.

48. Johnson, *Journey*, p. 40.

49. Grant, *Everyday Life on an Old Highland Farm*, p. 123.

50. Lawrence H. Gipson, *Great Britain and Ireland* ("The British Empire before the American Revolution," I [Caldwell, Idaho: Caxton Printers, Ltd., 1936]), pp. 192-93.

51. Robert Louis Stevenson, *Kidnapped* (Chicago: Scott, Foresman & Co., 1921), p. 184.

52. Basil Williams, *The Whig Supremacy, 1714-1760* (Oxford: Clarendon Press, 1949), p. 267.

53. Johnson, *Journey*, p. 77.

54. Selkirk, *Observations*, p. 20.

55. Johnson, *Journey*, p. 85.

56. *Some Eighteenth Century Tracts*, p. 430.

57. Johnson, *Journey*, p. 138.

58. *Ibid.*, p. 51.

59. *A List of the Persons Concerned in the Rebellion*, ed. The Earl of Rosebery (Edinburgh: T. & A. Constable, 1890), p. 360.

60. P. Hume Brown, *History of Scotland* (Cambridge, England: University Press, 1909), III, 303.

61. *Ibid.*, p. 316.

62. Agnes Mure Mackenzie, *Scotland in Modern Times, 1720-1939* (London: W. & R. C. Chambers, Ltd., 1941), p. 43; *Culloden Papers*, pp. 154-55.

63. *Journal of a Lady of Quality*, p. 34.

64. *Some Eighteenth Century Tracts*, p. 434.

65. *Ibid.*, pp. 436, 443.

66. *Scots Magazine*, XXXVI (February, 1774), 64.

67. "Records of Emigrants from England and Scotland to North Carolina," *North Carolina Historical Review*, XI (April, 1934), 138.

68. *Ibid.*, p. 131.

69. *The Jacobite Relics of Scotland*, pp. 185-86.

70. Donald F. MacDonald, *Scotland's Shifting Population, 1770-1850* (Glasgow: Jackson, Son & Co., 1937), p. 14.

71. Sir Walter Scott, *Rob Roy* (*Waverley Novels*, I [New York: Collier Publisher, n.d.]), p. 35.

72. Selkirk, *Observations*, p. 115.

73. *Forfeited Estates Papers*, pp. 61, 83, 159.

74. *Ibid.*, p. 85; Pennant, *A Tour in Scotland*, III, 91.

75. *Ibid.*, I, 204.

76. Johnson, *Journey*, p. 63.

77. Pennant, *A Tour in Scotland*, I, 204.

78. Sinclair, *General Report*, II, 405-8.

79. Johnson, *Journey*, p. 24.

80. Pennant, *A Tour in Scotland*, II, 11; III, 36, 112; Dunn, *Highland Settler*, p. 12.

81. As quoted in Grant, *Everyday Life on an Old Highland Farm*, p. 106.

82. Burt, *Letters*, II, 198-99.

83. *Scottish Population Statistics Including Webster's Analysis of Population 1755*, ed. James Gray Kyd (*Publications of the Scottish History Society*, Third Series, XLIII [Edinburgh: T. & A. Constable, 1952]), pp. xv, 7-8.

84. Sir John Sinclair, *The Statistical Account of Scotland* (Edinburgh: William Creech, 1790-98), XX, xiii-xix.

85. The statistics in Figure I are from *Scottish Population Statistics*, pp. 11-77, and Sinclair, *The Statistical Account*, XX, 587-621. The shires of Banff, Dumbarton, Elgin, Nairn, and Perth are only partly within the Highland Line. In determining the Highland parishes in these divided shires, the Earl of Selkirk apparently excludes several Aberdeen parishes from the Highland group on the basis of language. See Selkirk, *Observations*, pp. lix-lx. Between the years 1755 and 1781, several changes in parish lines occurred. These changes forced Sir John Sinclair to rework Webster's statistics in order to be able to compare populations in the same areas in 1755 and 1791. Such parish changes occurred in the shires of Argyll, Inverness, and Ross. In Figure I the statistics for these shires in 1755 are taken from Sinclair.

86. Thomas Pennant has left us an incomplete set of population statistics for twenty-two parishes in the year 1772, which statistics, when compared with Webster's 1755 figures, show a population loss of 3138. See Pennant, *A Tour in Scotland*, III, 441. Pennant records a population drop in fourteen of the twenty-two parishes. However, his figures are subject to suspicion. He often gives round numbers; 46 per cent of the numbers he gives are rounded to an even hundred. Pennant also give statistics for islands he "sailed by." For these reasons Pennant's population figures are disregarded in this study.

87. Thomas Garnett's and John Knox's statistics are quoted from Margaret I. Adam, "The Highland Emigration of 1770," *Scottish Historical Review*, XVI (July, 1919), 280-82.

88. Selkirk, *Observations*, p. 115.

89. Consult the *Scots Magazine, Glasgow Journal,* and *Edinburgh Evening Courant,* for the 1760's and 1770's.

90. Selkirk, *Observations*, pp. 56-60; Stanley C. Johnson, *A History of Emigration from the United Kingdom to North America, 1763-1912* (London: George Routledge & Sons, Ltd., 1913), pp. 1-2.

91. *Edinburgh Advertiser*, XXIII (January 3, 1775), 9.

92. *Forfeited Estates Papers*, pp. 62, 120-21, 236-37.

93. Margaret I. Adam, "Eighteenth Century Highland Landlords and the Poverty Problem," *Scottish Historical Review*, XIX (October, 1921), 2; Selkirk, *Observations*, p. xli; *Forfeited Estates Papers*, p. 220.

94. *Scots Magazine*, XXXIV, (Appendix for 1772), 698; *Forfeited Estates Papers*, p. 121; Sinclair, *General Report*, II, 395, 399.

95. Margaret I. Adam, "Eighteenth Century Landlords and the Poverty Problem," *Scottish Historical Review*, XIX (April, 1922), 169.

96. *Forfeited Estates Papers*, p. 225.

97. *Scots Magazine*, XXXVI (February, 1774), 64.

98. *Culloden Papers*, pp. 298, 301; *Forfeited Estates Papers*, p. 61.

99. "Records of Emigrants from England and Scotland to North Carolina, 1774-1775," *North Carolina Historical Review*, XI (April, 1934), 135.

100. *Ibid.,* p. 133.

101. *Scots Magazine*, XXXVII (December, 1775), 690.

102. *Edinburgh Advertiser*, XXI (January 4, 1774), 4.

CHAPTER IV

1. *The Jacobite Relics of Scotland,* collected and illustrated by James Hogg (Paisley: Alexander Gardner, 1874), p. 171.

2. *Scots Magazine* XXX (August, 1768), 446; XXXIII (June, 1771), 324; XXXIII (September, 1771), 33.

3. *Scots Magazine,* XXXIV (July, 1772), 395; XXXVI (April, 1774), 221. The second citation refers to the near starvation of another group of Highlanders, but their unfortunate situation was the result of shipwreck.

4. *Edinburgh Evening Courant,* September 1, 1773, *ap.,* Angus W. McLean MSS. (North Carolina Archives, Raleigh), pp. 59-60.

5. *Scots Magazine,* XXXIV (September, 1772), 515.

6. James Hogg Papers, "Answers and Defence for James Hogg," November 5, 1773 (Southern Historical Collection, Chapel Hill, North Carolina).

7. [Janet Schaw], *Journal of a Lady of Quality . . .,* eds. Evangeline W. Andrews and Charles McLean Andrews (New Haven: Yale University Press, 1921), pp. 49-51; *Colonial Records of North Carolina,* ed. William L. Saunders (Raleigh: State Printer, 1886-90), IV, 489.

8. The records of William Mackintosh, a tacksman, indicated that while his herd annually averaged fifty head, his tenants had only five head of cattle apiece. Isabel F. Grant, *Everyday Life on an Old Highland Farm, 1769-1782* (London: Longmans, Green and Co., 1924), pp. 61-62, 108-9.

9. James Hogg Papers, "Letter from the Reverend Alexander Pope to James Hogg." May 13, 1774, Southern Historical Collection, Chapel Hill, North Carolina.

10. Loyalist Papers, Auditor's Office, Class 13, Bundle 122 (North Carolina Archives, Raleigh).

11. The Earl of Selkirk, *Observations on the Present State of the Highlands of Scotland* (Edinburgh: A. Constable and Co., 1806), p. 159.

12. *Ibid.,* pp. 58-60. Many from this class, lacking funds to sail to America, moved to the Lowlands instead.

13. *Glasgow Journal,* March 28, 1771, *ap.* Angus W. McLean MSS (North Carolina Archives, Raleigh), p. 56.

14. James Hogg Papers, "Answers and Defence for James Hogg," November 5, 1773 (Southern Historical Collection, Chapel Hill, North Carolina).

15. *Glasgow Journal,* March 28, 1771, *ap.* Angus W. McLean MSS. (North Carolina Archives, Raleigh), p. 56.

16. Selkirk, *Observations,* p. 148.

17. James Hogg Papers, "Answers and Defence for James Hogg," November 5, 1773 (Southern Historical Collection, Chapel Hill, North Carolina).

18. Selkirk, *Observations,* p. 149.

19. James Hogg Papers, "Contract between James Hogg and James

Inglis, Jr.," August 24, 1773 (Southern Historical Collection, Chapel Hill, North Carolina).

20. Margaret I. Adam, "The Highland Emigration of 1770," *Scottish Historical Review*, XVI (July, 1919), 292.

21. Grant, *Everyday Life on an Old Highland Farm*, pp. 147-49.

22. *Edinburgh Advertiser*, XXI (March 11, 1774), 157.

23. "Records of Emigrants from England and Scotland to North Carolina, 1774-1775," *North Carolina Historical Review*, XI (January, 1934), 39-54, 129-43.

24. *The Lyon in Mourning*, ed. Robert Forbes (Edinburgh: University Press, 1896), III, 259.

25. *Scots Magazine*, XXXVI (February, 1774), 64.

26. This list is constructed from emigration reports in the *Scots Magazine, Edinburgh Evening Courant, Glasgow Journal, Edinburgh Advertiser, The Lyon in Mourning, Journal of a Lady of Quality*, Samuel Johnson's *Journey to the Western Islands of Scotland*, "Records of Emigrants from England and Scotland to North Carolina, 1774-1775," and Thomas Pennant's *A Tour in Scotland*. An attempt has been made to avoid duplication of reports, but since some notices are incomplete it is possible that several groups are listed twice.

27. This figure is based on the same sources used to construct Figure II. The number of items in this figure is smaller because some publications make no mention of the place of departure.

28. Samuel Johnson, *Journey to the Western Islands of Scotland* (Oxford: Oxford University Press, 1924). pp. 86-87.

29. James Hogg Papers, "Letter from the Reverend Alexander Pope to James Hogg," May 13, 1774 (Southern Historical Collection, Chapel Hill, North Carolina).

30. Johnson, *Journey*, p. 53. According to John P. MacLean's *An Historical Account of the Settlements of Scotch Highlanders in America Prior to the Peace of 1783* (Cleveland: Helman-Taylor Co., 1920), p. 108, one Highland dance song popular at the time included the words "Going to seek a fortune in North Carolina."

31. James Boswell, "Journal of a Tour to the Hebrides with Samuel Johnson," in Samuel Johnson, *Journey to the Western Islands of Scotland*, p. 346.

32. *Edinburgh Advertiser*, XXIII (May 26, 1775), 349.

33. Johnson, *Journey*, p. 87; *Scots Magazine*, XXXIII (June, 1771), 324.

34. *Colonial Records of North Carolina*, VIII, 620-21.

35. *Edinburgh Evening Courant*, September 29, 1773, *ap.* Angus W. McLean MSS., (North Carolina Archives, Raleigh), p. 60.

36. *Forfeited Estates Papers*, ed. A. H. Millar (Edinburgh: University Press, 1909), p. 120.

37. *Scots Magazine*, XXXV (December, 1773), 667.

38. *Ibid.*, XXXVII (September, 1775), 523.

39. John Knox's and Thomas Garnett's statistics are quoted from Margaret I. Adam, "Highland Emigration of 1770," *Scottish Historical Review*, XVI (July, 1919), 280-82.

40. *Ibid.*, p. 282.

41. *Scots Magazine*, 1768-1775, *passim.*

42. *Some Eighteenth Century Tracts Concerning North Carolina*, ed. William K. Boyd (Raleigh: Edwards and Broughton Co., 1927), p. 424; *Scots Magazine*, XXXVI (April, 1774), 221; "Records of Emigrants from England and Scotland to North Carolina, 1774-1775," *North Carolina Historical Review*, XI (April, 1934), 130-38; Ian C. C. Graham, *Colonists from Scotland: Emigration to North America, 1707-1783* (Ithaca: Cornell University Press, 1956), pp. 185-89.

43. Selkirk, *Observations*, p. 151.

44. *Scots Magazine*, XXXVI (March, 1774), 157-58.

45. *Journal of a Lady of Quality*, chapters I and II, especially pp. 71-72.

46. Alexander Mackenzie, *History of the Highland Clearance* (Glasgow: Jackson, Son & Co., n.d.), pp. 265-66.

47. James Hogg Papers, "Memorandum," October 20, [probably 1773] (Southern Historical Collection, Chapel Hill, North Carolina).

48. "Letter from James Oglethorpe to Duncan Forbes," *Culloden Papers*, ed. Duncan Forbes (London: T. Cadell & W. Davies, 1815), p. 155.

49. *Scots Magazine*, XXXVII (December, 1775), 690.

50. *Documents Relative to the Colonial History of New York*, ed. E. B. O'Callaghan (Albany, N. Y.: State of New York, 1853), VII, 629-31.

51. *Scots Magazine*, XXXV (September, 1773), 499.

52. *Ibid.*, XXXVI (August and March, 1774), 446, 157-58; Selkirk, *Observations*, p. 172.

53. *Documents Relative to the Colonial History of New York*, VIII, 682-83.

54. *Scots Magazine*, XXX (August, 1768), 446, 379.

55. Charles W. Dunn, *Highland Settler: A Portrait of the Scottish Gael in Nova Scotia* (Toronto: University of Toronto Press, 1953), p. 13. MacLean, *An Historical Account of the Settlements*, pp. 231-32.

56. Mackenzie, *History of the Highland Clearance*, pp. 265-66.

57. Selkirk, *Observations*, p. 173.

58. *Scots Magazine*, XXX-XXXVIII (1768-1775), *passim.*

CHAPTER V

1. Sir Walter Scott, *Waverley* (Philadelphia: Porter and Coats, n.d.), p. 92.

2. John S. Bassett, "The Influence of Coast Line and Rivers on North Carolina," *American Historical Association Annual Report*, I (1908), pp. 58-61. See Map II, which is adapted from the map on the last page of Charles C. Crittenden's *The Commerce of North Carolina, 1763-1789* (New Haven: Yale University Press, 1936).

3. *Colonial Records of North Carolina*, ed. William L. Saunders (Raleigh: State Printer, 1886-90), II, x.

4. *Ibid.*, V, 158. At low tide the depth was only nine and a half feet. [Janet Schaw], *Journal of a Lady of Quality*, eds. Evangeline W. and Charles M. Andrews (New Haven: Yale University Press, 1921), p. 279; "Robert Horne's Description of Carolina," *Narratives of Early Carolina*, ed. Alexander S. Sally (New York: Charles Scribner's Sons, 1911), p. 67.

5. Crittenden, *The Commerce of North Carolina*, pp. 9-10.

6. *Colonial Records of North Carolina*, II, 38-45, 47-48; "John Archdale's Description of Carolina," *Narratives of Early Carolina*, pp. 301-2.

7. *South Carolina Historical Society Collection* (Charleston: Privately printed, 1857), II, 235-37; Shirley C. Hughson, "The Carolina Pirates and Colonial Commerce, 1670-1740," *Johns Hopkins University Studies*, Twelfth Series (1894), pp. 330-46.

8. *Colonial Records of North Carolina*, II, xvi.

9. The Cape Fear River divided at Wilmington (originally known as Newton) into the Northeast Cape Fear River and the Northwest Cape Fear River. The latter is the longer and more important river. When the name Cape Fear River appears, it is always in reference to the Northwest Cape Fear. The Northeast Cape Fear River is usually known simply as the "Northeast."

10. *Colonial Records of North Carolina*, I, xii; II, 123.

11. William H. Foote in *Sketches of North Carolina* (New York: Robert Carter, 1846), p. 125, was the first to assert that Highlanders were living on the Cape Fear River in 1729. Foote visited the Highlander settlements often and in this matter he may have recorded what was their oral tradition. Foote's account is repeated in Charles A. Hanna, *The Scotch-Irish* (New York: G. P. Putnam's Sons, 1902), II, 33; John P. MacLean, *An Historical Account of the Settlements of Scottish Highlanders in America Prior to the Peace of 1783* (Cleveland: Helman-Taylor Co., 1920), p. 268; Hugh T. Lefler and Albert R. Newsome, *North Carolina: The History of a Southern State* (Chapel Hill: University of North Carolina Press, 1954), p. 72; and in most other histories that deal with the settlement.

12. North Carolina Land Grant Records (Secretary of State's Office, Raleigh), VII, 7, 8, 14, 20, 25. The incompleteness of land grant records in *Colonial Records of North Carolina* is demonstrated in the case of James Innes, since no grants are listed for him until 1735.

13. A few individuals secured land grants without personally proving their rights to the governor and council. In these instances the Board of Trade granted the land directly, often to friends or associates in England. Such grants were always large, amounting to thousands of acres. Henry McCulloh's grants of 60,000 and 70,000 acres are in this category. *Colonial Records of North Carolina*, IV, 685-98, 1083.

14. *Ibid.*, p. 4.

15. Samuel A'Court Ashe, *History of North Carolina* (Greensboro, N. C.: Charles L. Van Noppen, 1925), I, 253.

16. James Innes was named a member of the colonial council by

Governor Johnston in 1750. *Colonial Records of North Carolina,* IV, 1041-42.

17. *Ibid.,* III, 534.

18. *Ibid.,* IV, 490, 599.

19. "[Y]ou are to take especial care that no grant be made to any person but in proportion to his ability to cultivate the same. . . . And as the most probable measure for your judgment in this particular will be to proportion the quantity of land to the number of persons and slaves in each grantee's family, you are hereby directed not to grant to any person more than fifty acres for every white or black man, woman, or child of which the grantee's family shall consist at the time the grant shall be made." The above instructions applied in North Carolina from 1730 to 1754. *Royal Instructions to British Colonial Governors, 1670-1776,* ed. Leonard W. Labaree (New York: D. Appleton-Century Co., 1935), II, 565. In 1750 Governor Johnston informed the Board of Trade that "the Terms and conditions under which the land Warrents are granted can be no other than the number of Persons of which the Petitioners family consists." *Colonial Records of North Carolina,* IV, 1084.

20. During the period of settlement the frontier counties had few Negroes. *Ibid.,* III, 154-55; V, 320, 575, 603.

21. A discussion of the method used in determining the names of Highlanders appears later in this chapter. The following persons with Highland names received land grants in the designated years: 1734, John Lyon; 1735, Richard Dunn, John Dunn, Neil Gray, Alexander Legg, James Campbell, John Smith, Joseph Clark; 1736, John Macknight; 1737, William Gill, Alexander McDaniel, Magdaline Campbell. North Carolina Land Grant Records (Secretary of State's Office, Raleigh), III, VII, IX, *passim.* The name John Smith might well be considered an English name, but evidence from several sources indicates that this individual was a Highlander. Foote wrote of a John Smith who came to North Carolina in 1735 and settled among the Highlanders. According to Foote, Smith's wife, Margaret Gilchrist, died on the trip up the Cape Fear River, but two children, Malcolm and Janet, survived to aid him in his settlement. *Sketches of North Carolina,* p. 125. In May of 1735 a land grant was issued to John Smith for an acreage on the Cape Fear River. North Carolina Land Grant Records (Secretary of State's Office, Raleigh), III, 318. In the 1740's Malcolm Smith purchased land from James Innes, and in 1749 Malcolm Smith went to the council protesting that Hector McNeil, his neighbor, was claiming part of his land. *Colonial Records of North Carolina,* IV, 947. The Angus MacLean MSS (North Carolina Archives, Raleigh), pp. 174-80, stated that Janet Smith married into the McNeil family and five of her sons were Loyalist officers during the Revolution. Ronald M. Douglas indicated in *The Scots Book* (New York: The Macmillan Co., 1935), p. 184, that the name Smith was sometime used as the Anglicized form of the Gaelic name Mac a'Ghobbhainn by those who left the Highlands. The name Clark, which appeared in the 1735 list, is not commonly considered

a Highland name, although many of that name resided in Argyllshire and Perthshire. There were Clark septs in the Cameron, Mackintosh and Macpherson clans. Robert Bain, *The Clans and Tartans of Scotland* (London: Collins, n.d.), p. 18. As in the case of John Smith, Foote mentioned (p. 125) a Clark family that came to North Carolina from Argyllshire in the 1730's.

22. North Carolina Land Grant Records (Secretary of State's Office, Raleigh), VII, 15.

23. *Ibid.*, III, 291, 277, 278; VII, 8, 20. *Colonial Records of North Carolina*, IV, 947-48. Both Hammond Creek and Rockfish Creek are identified on Map V.

24. *Some Eighteenth Tracts Concerning North Carolina*, ed. William K. Boyd (Raleigh: Edwards and Broughton Co., 1927), p. 436; *Town and Country Magazine*, VIII (September, 1776), 470-71.

25. Edgar Bingham, *Physiographic Diagram of North Carolina* (New York: The Geographical Press, 1952), p. 1; *Hydrologic Data on the Cape Fear River Basin, 1820-1945*, ed. R. Bruce Ethridge (Washington: U. S. Geological Survey, 1947), pp. 3-5.

26. Lord Adam Gordon, "Journal of an Officer's Travels in America and the West Indies, 1764-1765," *Travel in the American Colonies*, ed. Newton D. Mereness (New York: Macmillan Co., 1916), p. 400.

27. Percival Perry, "The Naval Stores Industry in the Ante-Bellum South," (Unpublished dissertation, Duke University, Durham, N. C.), pp. iii, 5, 12.

28. John F. Smyth, *A Tour in the United States of America* (London: G. Robinson, 1784), II, 94; *Some Eighteenth Century Tracts*, p. 441.

29. *Journal of a Lady of Quality*, pp. 277-82; *Colonial Records of North Carolina*, III, xvi, 79-80, 119.

30. *Journal of a Lady of Quality*, p. 282.

31. *Colonial Records of North Carolina*, IV, 424.

32. *Ibid.*, 457-58.

33. *Journal of a Lady of Quality*, pp. 282-83.

34. *Colonial Records of North Carolina*, IV, 418.

35. James Hogg Papers, Contract between James Hogg and James Inglis, Jr., August 24, 1773 (Southern Historical Collection, Chapel Hill, North Carolina).

36. *Colonial Records of North Carolina*, III, 543-44.

37. *Edinburgh Advertiser*, March 22, 1776, *ap.* Angus McLean MSS. (North Carolina Archives, Raleigh), p. 62.

38. *Colonial Records of North Carolina*, IX, 659.

39. *Some Eighteenth Century Tracts*, p. 440.

40. *Records of the Moravians of North Carolina*, ed. Adelaide L. Fries (Raleigh: Edwards and Broughton, 1922, 1925, 1926), I, 40, 260-62; Crittenden, *The Commerce of North Carolina*, p. 18.

41. Conversation with Mr. John A. Oates, local historian, Fayetteville, North Carolina, September, 1954.

42. Land transfers registered in the Recorder's Office for Cumberland County, North Carolina, show that the first lots in the town of

Cross Creek were sold in 1760. See index of transfers for that year, "John Stephens, grantor, Richard Lyon, grantee."

43. *Colonial Records of North Carolina,* VI, 485-86, 815-16.

44. *Ibid.,* VII, 639; VIII, 295, 400; IX, 79-80.

45. Index of land transfers for Cumberland County 1760-1768 (Recorder's Office, Fayetteville, N. C.), *passim.*

46. *Records of the Moravians,* II, 593, 761-62; Crittenden, *The Commerce of North Carolina,* pp. 87-88.

47. *Colonial Records of North Carolina,* IX, 115, 395, 659; XXXIII, 439, 753-54, 870-71, 908-9, 918-19; XXV, 330.

48. Map III is an adaptation of a map on the last page of Crittenden's *Commerce of North Carolina,* and Henry Mouzon's "An Accurate Map of North and South Carolina with their Indian Frontiers . . .," 1775 (North Carolina Archives, Raleigh).

49. *Colonial Records of North Carolina,* IV, 489. Neal McNeal, one member of the party, had been called the leader of the emigration by John P. McLean in *An Historical Account of the Settlements,* p. 104. However, the above citation in the *Colonial Records of North Carolina* indicates that Dugald McNeil and "Coll" McAlister were the spokesmen for the group before the council and assembly.

50. *Colonial Records of North Carolina,* IV, 490.

51. *Ibid.,* 533.

52. *Ibid.,* 453-54. In Figure III the location of the James Fergus grant in New Hanover County must be an eighteenth-century clerical mistake. A surveyor's description of the plot shows that it was on the Cape Fear River eight miles above Rockfish Creek. This is clearly part of Bladen County. North Carolina Land Grants (Secretary of State's Officer, Raleigh), VIII, 76.

53. *Ibid.,* 70-76.

54. Map IV is adapted from maps on pp. 284-85 of David L. Corbitt's *Formation of North Carolina Counties, 1663-1943* (Raleigh: State Department of Archives and History, 1950).

55. *Colonial Records of North Carolina,* VI, 227; III, 425, 450.

56. *Ibid.,* IV, 887-89. The Granville line divided North Carolina at 35° 34' north parallel. Lord Granville, one of the original proprietors, refused to sell his interests to the crown when the colony was put under royal control in 1729. He was given proprietary rights to land sales and quitrents in that part of North Carolina above the Granville line.

57. *Ibid.,* V, 151.

58. *Scots Magazine,* XXX, 446; XXXI, 501, 602; XXXII, 457; XXXIII, 500; XXXIV, 395, 515.

59. *Colonial Records of North Carolina,* VIII, 526.

60. *Ibid.,* IX, 259.

61. Unfortunately the county population statistics in the "Lists of Taxables" are unreliable. *Ibid.,* V, 320; VII, 145, 283, 539-40.

62. *Ibid.,* X, 406-9.

63. Hugh F. Rankin, "The Moore's Creek Bridge Campaign, 1776," *North Carolina Historical Review,* XXX (January, 1953), 33.

64. *Colonial Records of North Carolina,* VII, 283-84.

65. *Ibid.,* IV, 1076.

66. *Ibid.,* pp. 601, 1083.

67. *Ibid.,* pp. 1090-91; V, 1132-33.

68. *Ibid.,* IV, 54.

69. *Ibid.,* I, 635.

70. *Ibid.,* III, 102.

71. *Ibid.,* IV, 685-95.

72. *Ibid.,* VII, 512, 543.

73. Writing about the North Carolina grantee, Charles L. Raper observed in his *North Carolina: A Study in English Colonial Government* (New York: Macmillan Co. 1904), p. 119, "He obtained his lands by making a small purchase payment and by pledging himself to pay an annual quitrent. . . ." During the period of royal administration, the instructions issued to the North Carolina governors made no provisions for the sale of land, and there are no records of land sales or the receipt of money from such sales. Marshall D. Harris in his work on the *Origin of the Land Tenure System in the United States* (Ames, Iowa: Iowa State College Press, 1953) has a section devoted to "Disposition of Land by Sale." In so much of this section as deals with North Carolina, he describes land sales in 1729 and 1777 but disregards the entire period of royal control in the colony (pp. 246-47). No doubt this procedure was necessary, because there is no evidence of land sales during those years. A Scottish visitor to the colony in the 1770's described the process of land granting but made no mention of sale of land by the crown. "Informations Concerning North Carolina," *Some Eighteenth Century Tracts,* p. 443. The fees associated with the grants were payment to royal officials (the governor, governor's secretary, auditor, surveyor, and attorney general) for their services. These fees were clearly identified as such and did not constitute a purchase payment. *Colonial Records of North Carolina,* IV, 770, 1128. In January, 1774, the Board of Trade instructed Governor Josiah Martin to cease granting land on the basis of headrights, and he was further ordered to have the remaining public lands surveyed. At the conclusion of the surveys, the lands were to be divided into units and offered at public sales. *Royal Instructions to British Colonial Governors,* II, 533-37. Governor Martin immediately protested, "I confess, when I consider the purchase money to be paid, and the advance Quit Rent, together with the novelty of the scheme and the poverty of the People, with whom the Lands ungranted will be in request, I think it will have all the effects of an absolute interdict to grant the King's Lands here. . . ." *Colonial Records of North Carolina,* IX, 990. Thirteen months later Governor Martin was forced to flee the colony, thus ending royal administration in North Carolina. In this thirteen-month period the sale of crown lands did not begin, perhaps because the surveys were not yet complete. Meanwhile Governor Martin continued to grant lands on the basis of the old system. *Ibid.,* X, 324-25; North Carolina Land Grants (Secretary of State's Office, Raleigh), XXVI, *passim.*

74. *Colonial Records of North Carolina*, I, 556-696.

75. In 1774 the maximum fee for securing title to a plot of 640 acres was £10 in Public Bills of Credit. *Ibid.*, IV, 712. The exchange rate between North Carolina Bills of Credit and sterling was ten to one. *Records of the Moravians*, II, 629.

76. *Journal of a Lady of Quality*, pp. 54-55.

77. *Colonial Records of North Carolina*, IX, 364.

78. "Records of Emigrants from England and Scotland to North Carolina, 1774-1775," *North Carolina Historical Review*, XI (April, 1934), 135, 138.

79. A few grants were not registered because of clerical oversight and several pages are mutilated, but the omissions are remarkably few for a collection of thirty-seven volumes of colonial grants.

80. In determining Highland and Lowland names, Bain's *The Clans and Tartans of Scotland* and Douglas' *The Scots Book* were consulted.

81. For example of this, compare the entries for families such as the Campbells or Monroes in the Cumberland County Recorder's Index Book and in the Index of Land Grants in the Secretary of State's Office in Raleigh. Instances of land purchases predating land grants to the same name are infrequent.

82. *State Records of North Carolina* (Winston, Goldsboro, Charlotte, N. C.: State Printers, 1895-1905), XXVI, 437-64.

83. Angus W. McLean MSS. (North Carolina Archives, Raleigh), p. 82.

84. North Carolina Land Grants (Secretary of State's Office, Raleigh), V, 426.

85. *Ibid.*, XIII, 46, 119; XX, 495; XXII, 196.

86. The South River before 1775 was known as the Black River on the Mouzon and Collet maps (North Carolina Archives, Raleigh).

CHAPTER VI

1. *Ancient Ballads and Songs of the North of Scotland*, ed. Peter Buchan (Edinburgh: W. and D. Laring, 1828), II, 148.

2. *Some Eighteenth Century Tracts Concerning North Carolina*, ed. William K. Boyd (Raleigh: Edwards and Broughton Co., 1927), p. 449.

3. Hector McNeil operated a sawmill in 1761. "Will of Hector McNeil, 1761," Cumberland County Collection (North Carolina Archives, Raleigh); Robert D. W. Connor, *North Carolina: Rebuilding an Ancient Commonwealth, 1584-1925* (Chicago: Lewis Publishing Co., 1929), I, 187.

4. *Some Eighteenth Century Tracts*, pp. 441-44.

5. John F. Smyth, *A Tour in the United States of America* (London: G. Robinson, 1784), I, 94. Smyth visited North Carolina during the Revolution.

6. [Janet Schaw], *Journal of a Lady of Quality*, eds. Evangeline W. and Charles M. Andrews (New Haven: Yale University Press, 1921), p. 164.

7. In the State Archives at Raleigh are seven inventories of estates and twenty-two wills that refer to the estates of Highlanders in Cumberland County. Only one of the inventories lists a plow (Neil Buie), but five of the seven inventories list hoes and another simply refers to "plantation tools." The will of Archibald McKay speaks of "plow horses," so presumably he had a plow, too.

8. "Inventory of Estate of Neil Buie, 1761," Cumberland County Collection (North Carolina Archives, Raleigh).

9. *Journal of a Lady of Quality,* p. 281; *Some Eighteenth Century Tracts,* p. 441.

10. *American Husbandry,* ed. Harry J. Carman (New York: Columbia University Press, 1939), p. 242.

11. Smyth, *A Tour in the United States,* I, 94; *American Husbandry,* p. 242.

12. *Journal of a Lady of Quality,* p. 160.

13. *Colonial Records of North Carolina,* ed. William L. Saunders (Raleigh: State Printer, 1886-90), IV, 220.

14. *Ibid.,* VI, 1029-30.

15. "Will of John Campbell," "Will of Hector McNeil, 1761," Cumberland County Collection (North Carolina Archives, Raleigh).

16. Loyalist Papers, Auditor's Office, Class 13, Bundle 122 (North Carolina Archives, Raleigh).

17. *Colonial Records of North Carolina,* III, 148-49; Smyth, *A Tour in the United States,* I, 143; *American Husbandry,* p. 241.

18. "Will of Jeane Campbell, 1765," Cumberland County Collection (North Carolina Archives, Raleigh).

19. "Inventory of Neill McNeill's Estate, 1766," Cumberland County Collection (North Carolina Archives, Raleigh).

20. Smyth, *A Tour in the United States,* I, 143.

21. *American Husbandry,* p. 241.

22. *Some Eighteenth Century Tracts,* p. 445. The will of John McFarland identifies his stock by the brand assigned to him. "Will of John McFarland, 1767," Cumberland County Collection (North Carolina Archives, Raleigh).

23. *Town and Country Magazine,* VI (1774), 566.

24. *American Husbandry,* p. 241.

25. Cumberland County Collection (North Carolina Archives, Raleigh).

26. *Second Report of the Bureau of Archives for the Province of Ontario, 1904,* ed. Alexander Fraser (Toronto: L. K. Cameron, 1905), Part I, 96, 550.

27. Smyth, *A Tour in the United States,* II, 78.

28. Angus W. McLean MSS. (North Carolina Archives, Raleigh), p. 82; Lewis C. Gray, *History of Agriculture in the Southern United States to 1860* (Washington, D. C.: The Carnegie Institute of Washington, 1933), I, 204-5. On the same page Gray writes about the term *black cattle* as follows: "It is probable that the term *black cattle* came to be used in a generic sense as a synonym for cattle, due to the wide-

spread prevalence of black cattle derived from the importations of the early colonial period."

29. *Colonial Records of North Carolina*, VI, 1030; *American Husbandry*, p. 242.

30. Percival Perry, "The Naval Stores Industry in the Ante-Bellum South," (Unpublished dissertation, Duke University, Durham, N. C.), p. iii.

31. "Inventory of Estate of John Rutherfurd, 1782," Cumberland County Collection (North Carolina Archives, Raleigh). This family name was sometimes spelled Rutherford in the eighteenth century.

32. *Some Eighteenth Century Tracts*, p. 448.

33. "Will of Andrew Armour, 1792," "Will of Neil Buie, 1761," "Inventory of Estate of Neil Buie, 1761," Cumberland County Collection (North Carolina Archives, Raleigh).

34. *State Records of North Carolina* (Winston, Goldsboro, Charlotte; N. C.: State Printers, 1895-1905), XXVI, 437-64, *passim*.

35. Loyalist Papers, Auditor's Office, Class 13, Bundle 22 (North Carolina Archives, Raleigh).

36. *State Records of North Carolina*, XXIII, 63, 169.

37. "Will of Duncan Brown, 1761," "Will of Neil McNeil, 1762," "Will of John McFarland, 1767," "Cumberland County Collection (North Carolina Archives, Raleigh).

38. *Colonial Records of North Carolina*, V, 603.

39. *State Records of North Carolina*, XXVI, 437-64, *passim*.

40. Rosser H. Taylor, *Slaveholding in North Carolina: an Economic View* ("James Sprunt Historical Studies," XVIII [Chapel Hill: University of North Carolina Press, 1926]), p. 18-19.

41. *State Records of North Carolina*, XXVI, 437-64, *passim*.

42. *Scots Magazine*, XXXIII (June, 1771), p. 324.

43. *Records of the Moravians in North Carolina*, ed. Adelaide L. Fries (Raleigh: Edwards and Broughton Co., 1922, 1925, 1926), II, 561-72.

44. *Journal of a Lady of Quality*, p. 175.

45. *Records of the Moravians*, II, 577-80.

46. "Inventory of Estate of Neill Buie, 1761," Cumberland County Collection (North Carolina Archives, Raleigh).

47. *Records of the Moravians*, II, 580.

48. *State Records of North Carolina*, XXVI, 437-64; Angus W. McLean MSS (North Carolina Archives, Raleigh), p. 82. McEachin was Governor Angus McLean's great-great-grandfather.

49. Samuel Johnson, *Journey to the Western Islands of Scotland* (Oxford: Oxford University Press, 1924), p. 73; "Records of the Emigrants from England and Scotland to North Carolina, 1774-1775," *North Carolina Historical Review*, XI (April, 1934), 48, 132, 135, 137.

50. *State Records of North Carolina*, XV, 209.

51. *Records of the Moravians*, II, 762, 884, 891, 910; Christopher C. Crittenden, *The Commerce of North Carolina, 1763-1789* (New Haven: Yale University Press, 1936), pp. 90, 100-1.

52. "An Inventory of the Amount the Estate of John Rutherfurd owed the Estate of Robert Hogg, 1782," Cumberland County Collection (North Carolina Archives, Raleigh).

53. *Records of the Moravians*, II, 706.

54. *Ibid.*, I, 307.

55. *Ibid.*, II, 762.

56. *Some Eighteenth Century Tracts*, p. 448.

57. "Nov. 29, 1775 . . . Our trade is now largely with Cross Creek, where salt especially can be secured." *Records of the Moravians*, II, 891, 893.

58. *Ibid.*, III, 1058; *Colonial Records of North Carolina*, X, 704.

59. "Will of William Campbell, 1774," Cumberland County Collection (North Carolina Archives, Raleigh); *Colonial Records of North Carolina*, X, 438, 643; *State Records of North Carolina*, XXVI, 458-64; Crittenden, *The Commerce of North Carolina*, pp. 96, 103.

60. Loyalist Papers, Auditor's Office, Class 12, Bundle 34 (North Carolina Archives, Raleigh), pp. 129-42, 163-79.

61. Loyalist Papers, Auditor's Office, Class 13, Bundle 122.

62. Records of Land Transfers in Cumberland County 1754-1775, Index Book (Recorder's Office, Fayetteville, N. C.).

63. *Scottish Population Statistics including Webster's Analysis of Population 1755*, ed. James Gray Kyd ("Publications of the Scottish Historical Society," Third Series, XLIII [Edinburgh: T. and A. Constable, 1952]), p. 35; Richard Pococke, *Tours in Scotland* (Edinburgh: University Press, 1887), p. 93.

64. Wallace Notestein, *The Scot in History* (New Haven: Yale University Press, 1947), p. 200.

65. *Scottish Population Statistics*, p. 35; Pococke, *Tours in Scotland*, p. 93.

66. "Minutes of Inverary Presbytery," November 3, 1741, *ap.* Charles A. Briggs, *American Presbyterianism* (New York: Scribner, 1885), pp. 292-93.

67. *Ibid.*

68. Hugh McAden's Journal has been lost, but parts of it are quoted in William Henry Foote's *Sketches of North Carolina* (New York: Robert Carter, 1846). For the above sections, see p. 171.

69. *Ibid.*, p. 132.

70. "Contract with Reverend James Campbell," Book A, p. 349 (Recorder's Office, Fayetteville, N. C.).

71. The following signed the contract: Hector McNeill, Gilbert Clark, Thomas Gibson, Alexander McAlister, Malcolm Smith, Archibald McKay, John Patterson, Dushee Shaw, Neill McNeill, Archibald Buie, Anguish McPherson. Witnesses to the signing were Archibald McNeill and Archibald Clark.

72. Cumberland County Records, January session, 1759 (Recorder's Office, Fayetteville, N. C.); Samuel A' Court Ashe, *History of North Carolina* (Greensboro, N. C.: Charles L. Van Noppen, 1925), I, 387.

73. *Colonial Records of North Carolina*, VI, 881.

74. *Ibid.*, VIII, 527; IX, 285, 682.

75. Neill McKay, *A Centenary Sermon* (Fayetteville, N. C.: Presbyterian Office, 1858), pp. 8-9; James Banks, *A Centennial Historical Address* (Fayetteville, N. C.: Presbyterian Office, 1858), 12-15.

76. *The Lyon in Mourning*, ed. Robert Forbes (Edinburgh: University Press, 1896), III, 259.

77. *Colonial Records of North Carolina*, V, 1196, 1198; X, 577.

78. Donald McDonald, "A History of Barbecue Church in Harnett County, North Carolina," (Typewritten manuscript, University of North Carolina Library, Chapel Hill, N. C.), p. 13.

79. This refers to those individuals who fall in the three categories discussed in chapter v.

80. Records of Land Transfers, 1754-1775, Index Book (Recorder's Office, Fayetteville, N. C.).

81. *Colonial Records of North Carolina*, IX, 79-80, 684.

82. This map is adapted from a map in Ashe, *History of North Carolina*, I, 376.

83. Guion G. Johnson, *Ante-Bellum North Carolina* (Chapel Hill: University of North Carolina Press, 1937), 8-12.

84. Records of Land Transfers 1754-1775, Index Book (Recorder's Office, Fayetteville, N. C.).

85. Johnson, *Journey*, pp. 31, 48, 51, 80.

86. *Colonial Records of North Carolina*, VII, 351; IX, 451, 473.

87. Johnson, *Journey*, p. 51.

88. *Ibid.*, pp. 51, 104-6; Charles W. Dunn, *Highland Settler: A Portrait of the Scottish Gael in Nova Scotia* (Toronto: University of Toronto Press, 1953), p. 34.

89. *Ibid.*, p. 138.

90. *Ibid.*

91. *North Carolina Wills and Inventories*, ed. J. Bryan Grimes (Raleigh: Edwards and Broughton Printing Co., 1912), p. 265.

92. *Colonial Records of North Carolina*, V, xvii; *State Records of North Carolina*, XXIV, 511-13.

93. "Will of Malcolm Blue, 1764," Cumberland County Collection (North Carolina Archives, Raleigh).

94. "Will of Patrick Campbell, 1775," Cumberland County Collection (North Carolina Archives, Raleigh).

95. *Colonial Records of North Carolina*, V, 1219, 1225.

96. "Records of Emigrants from England and Scotland to North Carolina, 1774-1775," *North Carolina Historical Review*, XI (April, 1934), 136.

97. *Colonial Records of North Carolina*, X, 594-603.

98. North Carolina Land Grants (Secretary of State's Office, Raleigh), XXII, 337; see "Hugh McDonald 1775," "Donald McDonald 1774," "Angus McDonald 1774," Records of Land Transfers, 1754-1775, Index Book (Cumberland County Recorder's Office, Fayetteville, N. C.); Angus W. McLean MSS. (North Carolina Archives, Raleigh), pp. 105-7.

99. Loyalist Papers, Auditor's Office, Class 13, Bundle 122 (North Carolina Archives, Raleigh).

100. *Colonial Records of North Carolina*, X, 441-42.

101. Loyalist Papers, Auditor's Office, Class 13, Bundle 122 (North Carolina Archives, Raleigh).

102. *State Records of North Carolina*, XIII, 64-65.

103. *Colonial Records of North Carolina*, X, 346.

104. *Ibid.*, VIII, 144; VII, 618.

105. *Ibid.*, IX, 259.

106. *Ibid.*, p. 1159.

107. Guion G. Johnson, *Ante-Bellum North Carolina*, pp. 722-24.

108. *Records of the Moravians*, I, 334.

109. *Ibid.*, II, 616.

110. *The Gaelic Bards from 1715 to 1765*, ed. Reverend Alexander MacLean, p. 258, as quoted and translated in Dunn, *Highland Settler*, p. 27.

111. *Journal of a Lady of Quality*, p. 287.

112. *Colonial Records of North Carolina*, XXVI, 437-64.

113. "Records of Emigrants from England and Scotland to North Carolina, 1774-1775," *North Carolina Historical Review*, XI (April, 1934), 129-43.

114. *Journal of a Lady of Quality*, p. 157.

115. John A. Oates, *The Story of Fayetteville and the Upper Cape Fear* (Fayetteville, N. C.: Privately printed, 1950), pp. 821-23. The biographical sketch of Campbell which Oates has included in his book is a well-written piece by a descendent of Campbell.

116. "Records of Emigrants from England and Scotland to North Carolina, 1774-1775," *North Carolina Historical Review*, XI (April, 1934), p. 133.

117. "Will of John McFarland, 1767," Cumberland County Collection (North Carolina Archives, Raleigh).

118. "Will of Patrick Campbell, 1775," Cumberland County Collection (North Carolina Archives, Raleigh).

119. *Colonial Records of North Carolina*, IV, 219, 274, 335, 336.

120. North Carolina Land Grants (Secretary of State's Office, Raleigh), XX, 530-731; XXIII, 73.

121. "Will of Alexander Macalester, 1796," Cumberland County Collection (North Carolina Archives, Raleigh). The name MacAlister is spelled several ways in eighteenth-century records.

122. Cumberland County Collection (North Carolina Archives, Raleigh).

123. *North Carolina Wills and Inventories*, pp. 478, 482-84; Robert D. W. Connor, *North Carolina: Rebuilding an Ancient Commonwealth*, I, 187-88. For an artist's drawing of a humble Highland hut, see Thomas Pennant's *Tour in Scotland* (London: Benjamin Write, 1790), II, 262.

124. "Inventory of Estate of Neill Buie, 1761," Cumberland County Collection (North Carolina Archives, Raleigh).

125. "Inventory of the Goods and Chattels of John Brown, 1761," Cumberland County Collection (North Carolina Archives, Raleigh).

126. "Inventory of Estate of Archibald Clark, 1766," Cumberland County Collection (North Carolina Archives, Raleigh).

127. *Second Report of Bureau of Archives of the Province of Ontario,* Part I, 550.

128. Loyalist Papers, Auditor's Office, Class 13, Bundle 122 (North Carolina Archives, Raleigh).

129. Isabel F. Grant, *Everyday Life on an Old Highland Farm, 1769-1782* (London: Longmans, Green & Co., 1924), p. 91.

130. Johnson, *Journey,* p. 91.

131. *Journal of a Lady of Quality,* p. 185.

132. Loyalist Papers, Auditor's Office, Class 13, Bundle 122 (North Carolina Archives, Raleigh).

133. *North Carolina Wills and Inventories,* pp. 482-84.

134. Johnson, *Journey,* pp. 27, 91-92; Edward Burt, *Letters from a Gentleman in the North of Scotland to His Friend in London,* ed. R. Jamieson (London: Ogle, Duncan & Co., 1754), II, 59; Grant, *Everyday Life on an Old Highland Farm,* pp. 119-20.

135. John Brickell, *The Natural History of North Carolina,* (1743), pp. 30-34, 37-44, *ap. North Carolina History Told by Contemporaries,* ed. Hugh Lefler (Chapel Hill: University of North Carolina Press, 1934), p. 63; Connor, *Rebuilding an Ancient Commonwealth,* I, 187-88.

136. *Second Report of the Bureau of Archives of the Province of Ontario,* Part I, 549.

137. Pennant, *Tour in Scotland,* II, 312. Pennant in 1772 found food in short supply in most of the Western Islands and near famine conditions in some. *Ibid.,* II, 200, 221, 244, 263.

138. *Colonial Records of North Carolina,* IV, 4.

139. *Ibid.,* XII, 330, 421.

140. *Ibid.,* 1041-42.

141. *Ibid.,* V, 124; "James Innes Will," *North Carolina Wills and Inventories,* p. 265.

142. *Colonial Records of North Carolina,* V, 128.

143. "James Innes Will," *North Carolina Wills and Inventories,* p. 265.

144. *Colonial Records of North Carolina,* IV, 447.

145. *Ibid.,* VI, 740.

146. *Ibid.,* p. 204.

147. *Ibid.,* VI, 662, 800, 1150; VII, 351; VIII, 106; IX, 137, 1042, 1188.

148. *Ibid.,* IX, 1178.

149. *Journal of a Lady of Quality,* p. 323.

150. James Hogg Papers, Letter from Rev. Alexander Pope to James Hogg, May 13, 1774 (Southern Historical Collection, Chapel Hill, N. C.).

151. *Second Report of the Bureau of Archives of the Province of Ontario,* Part I, 54.

152. *Colonial Records of North Carolina,* IX, 1129-31; X, 246, 256-61; State Records of North Carolina, XXVI, 151-52, 323.

153. *Colonial Records of North Carolina,* IX, 1122-25; X, 273-74.

154. *Ibid.,* 259.
155. *Ibid.,* 373-76.
156. *Ibid.,* XIX, 466.
157. *Ibid.,* XXV, 22.

CHAPTER VII

1. Sir Walter Scott, *Waverley* (Philadelphia: Porter and Coates, n. d.), p. 149.
2. *Colonial Records of North Carolina,* VI, 1261.
3. *Ibid.,* VII, 123-25.
4. *Ibid.,* pp. 172-78.
5. *Ibid.,* p. 173.
6. *Ibid.,* p. 198.
7. *Ibid.,* p. 114.
8. *Ibid.,* p. 125.
9. *Ibid.,* pp. 168a-168b.
10. *Ibid.,* pp. 187-88.
11. *Ibid.,* p. 89.
12. *Ibid.,* p. 90.
13. *Ibid.,* pp. 705, 710-11; VIII, 253-54, 258-64.
14. *Records of the Moravians in North Carolina,* ed. Adelaide L. Fries (Raleigh: Edwards and Broughton Co., 1922, 1925, 1926), II, 651-653.
15. *Colonial Records of North Carolina,* VIII, 708.
16. *Ibid.,* VII, 713.
17. *Ibid.,* VIII, 345-46.
18. *Ibid.,* VII, 807; VIII, 77.
19. *Ibid.,* VIII, 601, 608, 701; VII, 717.
20. *Records of the Moravians,* II, 652-53.
21. *Colonial Records of North Carolina,* IX, 142.
22. *Ibid.,* p. 1167.
23. *Ibid.,* pp. 563, 578.
24. *Ibid.,* pp. 230-34.
25. *Ibid.,* pp. 737-41.
26. *American Archives . . .,* ed. Peter Force (Fourth Series; Washington, D. C., 1837-46), I, 618.
27. "Letter of William Hooper to James Iredell dated August 5, 1774," *Life and Correspondence of James Iredell,* ed. Griffith J. McRee (New York: Peter Smith, 1949), p. 201.
28. *American Archives,* Fourth Series, I, 733, 737.
29. *Colonial Records of North Carolina,* IX, 1041-44.
30. *Ibid.,* p. 1047.
31. *Ibid.,* pp. 1151, 1166.
32. *Ibid.,* p. 1095.
33. *Ibid.,* p. 1178.
34. *Ibid.,* p. 697.
35. *Records of the Moravians,* II, 872.
36. *Ibid.,* II, 852; Hugh T. Lefler and Albert R. Newsome, *North*

Carolina: The History of a Southern State (Chapel Hill: University of North Carolina Press, 1954), pp. 191-92.

37. [Janet Schaw], *Journal of a Lady of Quality . . .*, eds. Evangeline W. Andrews and Charles M. Andrews (New Haven: Yale University Press, 1921), pp. 186-87.

38. Sir Henry Clinton, *The American Rebellion* (New Haven: Yale University Press, 1954), p. 26.

39. *Colonial Records of North Carolina*, IX, 1160-62, 1167.

40. *Journal of a Lady of Quality*, p. 192.

41. *Colonial Records of North Carolina*, IX, 1174; X, 46-47, 266-67, 324-28, 406.

42. *Ibid.*, X, 46-47.

43. Letter of Lord Townshend to Dartmouth, July 21, 1775 (Dartmouth Manuscripts, North Carolina Archives, Raleigh).

44. *American Archives*, Fourth Series, II, 974.

45. *Ibid.*, III, 75-76.

46. *Colonial Records of North Carolina*, X, 145-50.

47. *American Archives*, Fourth Series, III, 443-44.

48. *Journal of a Lady of Quality*, p. 193.

49. *American Archives*, Fourth Series, III, 40; *Colonial Records of North Carolina*, X, 317.

50. *Ibid.*, pp. 173-74.

51. *Ibid.*, p. 191.

52. *Town and Country Magazine*, VIII (June, 1776), 334.

53. *Journal of a Lady of Quality*, p. 281.

54. Letter of Alexander Schaw to the Earl of Dartmouth, November 18, 1775 (Dartmouth Manuscripts, North Carolina Archives, Raleigh).

55. *Colonial Records of North Carolina*, X, 397.

56. *Ibid.*, pp. 441-42.

57. *Journal of a Lady of Quality*, p. 193.

58. *American Archives*, Fourth Series, III, 40.

59. *Ibid.*, p. 76; *Colonial Records of North Carolina*, X, 65, 68.

60. *Ibid.*, pp. 266-67.

61. *American Archives*, Fourth Series, III, 40; *Colonial Records of North Carolina*, X, 317.

62. *Ibid.*, pp. 173-74.

63. Philip Davidson, *Propaganda and the American Revolution, 1763-1783* (Chapel Hill: University of North Carolina Press, 1941), pp. 90-91.

64. *Journals of the American Congress: From 1774 to 1788* (Washington, D. C.: Way and Gideon, 1823), I, 191-92.

65. Davidson, *Propaganda and the American Revolution*, p. 199.

66. *American Archives*, Fourth Series, III, 1649-51.

67. *Ibid.*, II, 1030; *Colonial Records of North Carolina*, X, 29-30.

68. *Ibid.*, p. 112.

69. *Ibid.*, pp. 594-95.

70. *American Archives*, Fourth Series, I, 733; *Colonial Records of North Carolina*, IX, 1178.

71. *Ibid.*, X, 165.

72. *Ibid.*, VI, 1150; IX, 1042.

73. *Ibid.*, VI, 800; IX, 450.

74. *Ibid.*, IX, 1042.

75. *Ibid.*, X, 207.

76. Donald McDonald, "A History of Barbecue Church in Harnett County, North Carolina," (Typewritten manuscript, University of North Carolina Library, Chapel Hill, N. C.), p. 13.

77. *Colonial Records of North Carolina*, X, 266-67.

78. *Ibid.*, p. 452.

79. George M. Wrong, *Canada and the American Revolution* (New York: Macmillan Co., 1935), pp. 281-83; Carl Wittke, *A History of Canada* (New York: Alfred A. Knopf, 1928), pp. 53-54; Edgar McInnis, *Canada: A Political and Social History* (New York: Rinehart & Co., Inc., 1947), pp. 149-51.

80. *Journals of the American Congress*, I, 290.

81. *Ibid.*, p. 41.

82. *Ibid.*, p. 75.

83. *Ibid.*

84. Wittke, *A History of Canada*, p. 53.

85. Samuel Johnson, *Journey to the Western Islands of Scotland* (Oxford: Oxford University Press, 1924), p. 88.

86. Basil Williams, *The Whig Supremacy* (Oxford: Clarendon Press, 1949), 267-68.

87. P. Hume Brown, *History of Scotland* (Cambridge: University Press, 1909), III, 352.

88. Johnson, *Journey*, p. 130.

89. Brown, *History of Scotland*, III, 352.

90. *Jacobite Songs and Ballads*, ed. G. S. Macquoid (London: Walter Scott Publishing Co., n.d.), p. 275.

91. *American Archives*, Fourth Series, VI, 686.

92. *Ibid.*, p. 647.

93. *American Archives . . .*, ed. Peter Force (Fifth Series; Washington, D. C., 1848-53), I, 214.

94. Leonard Trinterud, *The Forming of an American Tradition: a Re-examination of Colonial Presbyterianism* (Philadelphia: Westminster Press, 1949), p. 249.

95. Ian C. C. Graham, *Colonists from Scotland: Emigration to North America, 1707-1783* (Ithaca: Cornell University Press, 1956), pp. 152-53.

96. *Letters on the American Revolution, 1774-1776*, ed. Margaret Wheeler Willard (Boston: Houghton Mifflin Co., 1925), p. 334.

97. *American Archives*, Fourth Series, IV, 980-81.

98. *Colonial Records of North Carolina*, X, 443.

99. *Ibid.*, p. 452.

100. Sir Walter Scott, *Waverley*, p. 36.

101. *Some Eighteenth Century Tracts Concerning North Carolina*, ed. William K. Boyd (Raleigh: Edwards and Broughton Co., 1927), pp. 434-36.

102. *Colonial Records of North Carolina,* X, 324-28.

103. *American Archives,* Fourth Series, IV, 312-13.

104. *Royal Instructions to British Colonial Governors, 1670-1776,* ed. Leonard Labaree (New York: D. Appleton-Century Co., 1935), II, 621-23.

105. *Colonial Records of North Carolina,* X, 421.

106. *Town and Country Magazine,* VIII (June, 1776), 334.

107. *Colonial Records of North Carolina,* X, 476. For several interesting observations on this question, see Elisha P. Douglass, *Rebels and Democrats* (Chapel Hill: University of North Carolina Press, 1955), pp. 111-12.

108. *Colonial Records of North Carolina,* X, 722-23.

109. *Ibid.,* pp. 46-47.

110. *Ibid.*

111. *Ibid.,* pp. 324-28.

112. *Ibid.*

113. *The Ballad Book,* ed. Mac Edward Leach (New York: Harper and Brothers, 1955), p. 579.

114. *Colonial Records of North Carolina,* X, 406.

115. *Records of the Moravians,* III, 1092.

116. *Ibid.,* pp. 1026-48.

117. *Colonial Records of North Carolina,* X, 467-68.

118. *Records of the Moravians,* III, 1026.

119. *Journal of a Lady of Quality,* p. 281.

120. *American Archives,* Fourth Series, IV, 1129; *Colonial Records of North Carolina,* X, 452.

121. *Ibid.,* pp. 594-97.

122. *Ibid.,* p. 165; Robert O. DeMond, *The Loyalists in North Carolina During the Revolution* (Durham: Duke University Press, 1940), p. 81. DeMond presents a fine discussion of Campbell's activities.

123. *Colonial Records of North Carolina,* X, 165.

124. *Ibid.,* p. 165.

125. *Ibid.,* p. 443.

126. *Ibid.,* p. 491; *The Letter-Book of Captain Alexander McDonald* ("Collections of the New-York Historical Society for the Year 1882," II [New York: New-York Historical Society, 1883]), p. 265.

127. *Colonial Records of North Carolina,* X, 490.

128. *Ibid.,* p. 444.

129. *Ibid.,* pp. 465-68.

130. *Ibid.,* XI, 283.

131. *Ibid.,* X, 594-95.

132. *Ibid.,* pp. 406.

133. *Ibid.,* pp. 467-68.

134. *Ibid.,* XI, 284.

135. John F. Smyth, *A Tour in the United States of America* (London: G. Robinson, 1784), I, 230.

136. *The Letter-Book of Captain Alexander McDonald,* p. 265.

137. *Colonial Records of North Carolina,* X, 482-84.

138. *Ibid.*, pp. 485-86; XI, 283-85. For the best description of the battle, see Hugh F. Rankin's "The Moore's Creek Bridge Campaign in 1776," *North Carolina Historical Review,* XXX (January, 1953), 23-32.

139. *Life and Correspondence of James Iredell,* p. 278; *Colonial Records of North Carolina,* X, 550.

140. DeMond, *The Loyalists in North Carolina,* pp. 111, 119-22.

141. *Ibid.*, pp. 111-12.

142. *State Records of North Carolina,* ed. Walter Clark (Winston, Goldsboro, Charlotte, N. C.: State Printers, 1895-1905), XXIV, 11.

143. *Colonial Records of North Carolina,* XI, 534, 743, 790; XIII, 368; V, 1198.

144. *Ibid.*, XV, 324.

145. Clinton, *The American Rebellion,* pp. 28-29.

146. *Ibid.*, p. 268.

147. *The Jacobite Relics of Scotland,* collected and illustrated by James Hogg (Paisley: Alexander Gardner, 1874), p. 427.

BIBLIOGRAPHY

PRIMARY SOURCES

Manuscripts

Collet, John. "A Compleat Map of North Carolina from an Actual Survey." 1770. North Carolina Archives, Raleigh.

Cumberland County Collection. North Carolina Archives, Raleigh. [In this collection are numberous eighteenth-century wills and inventories of estates of Highlanders who lived in that county.]

Dartmouth Papers. North Carolina Archives, Raleigh. [This sizable collection includes many letters referring to the British plans for an invasion of North Carolina in 1776, as well as other letters dealing with the confiscation of Loyalist property.]

James Hogg Papers. Southern Historical Collection, Louis Round Wilson Library, Chapel Hill, N. C. [The papers which have been preserved are letters, business records, legal documents, and memorandums.]

Loyalist Claims. (Audit Office Records, Class 12, Vol. XXXV [1783-90].) Public Record Office in England. Copies of those claims which pertain to North Carolina are in the North Carolina Archives, Raleigh.

Mouzon, Henry. "An accurate Map of North and South Carolina with their Indian Frontiers . . . from Actual Surveys." 1775. North Carolina Archives, Raleigh.

North Carolina Land Grants. Vols. I-XXXVII. Secretary of State's Office, Raleigh. [In these volumes, which cover the colonial period, there are few omissions. The records are easily accessible and well preserved.]

Records of Land Transfers in Cumberland County. Recorder's Office, Fayetteville, N. C. [Beginning in the year 1754, the records are complete for the colonial period. They are indexed and available for research.]

Books

Abstract of North Carolina Wills, ed. J. Bryan Grimes. Raleigh, N. C.: E. M. Uzzell & Co., 1910.

An Abstract of North Carolina Wills from about 1760 to about 1800, ed. Fred A. Olds. Baltimore: Southern Book Co., 1954.

American Archives, ed. Peter Force. Fourth Series. 6 vols. Washington, D. C.: M. St. Clair Clarke, 1837-46.

American Archives, ed. Peter Force. Fifth Series. 3 vols. Washington, D. C.: M. St. Clair Clarke, 1848-1853.

American Husbandry, ed. Harry J. Carman. New York: Columbia University Press, 1939.

Ancient Ballads and Songs of the North of Scotland, ed. Peter Buchan. Vol. II. Edinburgh: D. Laring, 1828.

The Ballad Book, ed. MacEdward Leach. New York: Harper and Brothers, 1955.

Boswell, James. "A Tour to the Hebrides," in Samuel Johnson, *Journey to the Western Islands of Scotland.* Oxford: Oxford University Press, 1924.

Burt, Edward. *Letters from a Gentleman in the North of Scotland to His Friend in London,* ed. R. Jamieson. London: Ogle, Duncan & Co., 1754.

Clinton, Sir Henry. *The American Rebellion,* ed. William B. Willcox. New Haven: Yale University Press, 1954.

Colonial Records of North Carolina, ed. William L. Saunders. 10 vols. Raleigh, N. C.: State Printer, 1886-90. [This collection of records is large and touches on most phases of colonial life.]

Culloden Papers, ed. Duncan Forbes. London: T. Cadell & W. Davies, 1815.

Documents Relative to the Colonial History of the State of New York ed. E. B. O'Callaghan. Vol. VIII. Albany, N. Y.: State of New York, 1853.

Forfeited Estates Papers, ed. A. H. Millar. Edinburgh: University Press, 1909.

Hepburn, Thomas. *A Letter to a Gentleman from His Friend in Orkney.* Edinburgh: William Brown, 1885. [Original printing in 1757.]

Jacobite Minstrelsy with Notes Illustrative of the Text and Containing Historical Details in Relation to the House of

Stuart, From 1640 to 1784. Glasgow: Printed for Richard Griffin & Co., 1829.

The Jacobite Relics of Scotland, collected and illustrated by James Hogg. Paisley: Alexander Gardner, 1874.

Jacobite Songs and Ballads, ed. G. S. Macquoid. London: Walter Scott Publishing Co., n.d.

Johnson, Samuel. *Journey to the Western Islands of Scotland.* Oxford: Oxford University Press, 1924.

Journals of the American Congress: From 1774 to 1788. Vol. I. Washington, D. C.: Way & Gideon, 1823.

Journals of the House of Commons. Vol. XXV. London, 1759.

Letter-Book of Captain Alexander McDonald. ("Collections of the New-York Historical Society for the Year 1882," No. II.) New York: New-York Historical Society, 1883.

Letters of James Murray, Loyalist, ed. N. M. Tiffany. Boston: W. B. Clarke & Co., 1901.

Letters on the American Revolution, 1774-1776, ed. Margaret Wheeler Willard. Boston: Houghton Mifflin Co., 1925.

Life and Correspondence of James Iredell, ed. Griffith J. McRee. 2 vols. New York: reprint by Peter Smith, 1949.

A List of the Persons Concerned in the Rebellion, ed. The Earl of Rosebery. Edinburgh: T. and A. Constable, 1890.

The Lyon in Mourning, ed. Robert Forbes. 3 vols. Edinburgh: University Press, 1896. [The work is an extensive collection of documents relating to the Rebellion of 1745 and its aftermath.]

Narratives of Early Carolina, 1650-1708, ed. Alexander S. Sally, Jr. New York: Charles Scribner's Sons, 1911.

North and South Carolina Marriage Records, ed. William M. Clemens. New York: E. P. Dutton & Co., 1927.

North Carolina History Told by Contemporaries, ed. Hugh Talmage Lefler. Chapel Hill: University of North Carolina Press, 1934.

North Carolina Wills and Inventories, ed. J. Bryan Grimes. Raleigh: Edwards and Broughton Printing Co., 1912.

Origins of the Forty-Five, ed. Walter B. Blaikie. Edinburgh: T. and A. Constable, 1916.

Parliamentary History of England, ed. Thomas C. Hansard. Vols. XIII-XIV. London: Thomas C. Hansard, 1813.

Pennant, Thomas. *A Tour in Scotland.* 3 vols. London: Benjamin White, 1790.

Pococke, Richard. *Tours in Scotland.* Edinburgh: University Press, 1887.

Prisoners of the '45, eds. Sir Bruce Gordon Seton and Jean Gordon Arnot. 3 vols. Edinburgh: University Press, 1928.

Records of the Moravians in North Carolina, ed. Adelaide L. Fries. Vols. I-III. Raleigh: Edwards and Broughton Co., 1922, 1925, 1926. [These interesting records provide information about many phases of life in the backwoods of North Carolina.]

Royal Instructions to British Colonial Governors, 1670-1776, ed. Leonard W. Labaree. Vol. II. New York: D. Appleton-Century Co., 1935.

[Schaw, Janet.] *Journal of a Lady of Quality,* eds. Evangeline W. and Charles M. Andrews. New Haven: Yale University Press, 1921. [This is a delightful account of a trip to North Carolina on the eve of the American Revolution by an observant Scottish woman.]

Scottish Population Statistics Including Webster's Analysis of Population 1755, ed. James Gray Kyd. ("Publications of the Scottish History Society," Third Series, Vol. XLIII.) Edinburgh: T. and A. Constable, 1952.

Second Report of the Bureau of Archives for the Province of Ontario, 1904, ed. Alexander Fraser. Parts I-II. Toronto: L. K. Cameron, 1905. [The Loyalist Claims for many of the North Carolinians who fled to Canada are printed in these two volumes.]

Selkirk, The Earl of. *Observations on the Present State of the Highlands of Scotland.* Edinburgh: A. Constable and Co., 1806.

Sinclair, Sir John. *General Report of the Agricultural State and Political Circumstances of Scotland.* 5 vols. Edinburgh: A. Constable and Co., 1814.

———. *The Statistical Account of Scotland.* 20 vols. Edinburgh: William Creech, 1790-1798. [These volumes contain the census returns for all the parishes of Scotland as collected by Sinclair in the 1790's.]

Smyth, John F. *A Tour in the United States of America.* Vols. I-II. London: G. Robinson, 1784.

Some Eighteenth Century Tracts Concerning North Carolina, ed. William K. Boyd. Raleigh: Edwards and Broughton Co., 1927. [Included in this collection are a letter by James Hogg and an essay which circulated in Scotland, entitled "Informations Concerning the Province of North Carolina."]

South Carolina Historical Society Collections. Vol. II. Charleston: South Carolina Historical Society, 1857.

State Records of North Carolina, ed. Walter Clark. 16 vols. Winston, Goldsboro, Charlotte: State Printers, 1895-1905.

Travel in the American Colonies, ed. Newton D. Mereness. New York: Macmillan Co., 1916.

Newspapers and Periodicals

The Cape Fear Mercury, Wilmington, N. C., 1769-75.

The Edinburgh Advertiser, Vols. XXI-XXIV, 1774-75.

Gentleman's Magazine, London, Vol. XVI, July, 1746.

London Magazine, London, Vols. I-XXXV, 1732-67.

"Records of Emigrants from England and Scotland to North Carolina, 1774-1775," A. R. Newsome, ed., *North Carolina Historical Review*, Vol. XI (January and April, 1934), pp. 39-54, 129-143.

Scots Magazine, Edinburgh, Vols. I-XXXVIII, 1739-76.

Town and Country Magazine, London, Vols. I-VIII, 1769-76.

SECONDARY SOURCES

Manuscripts

McDonald, Donald. "A History of Barbecue Church in Harnett County, North Carolina." Unpublished typewritten manuscript, University of North Carolina Library, Chapel Hill, N. C., 1927.

McLean, Angus Wilton. "A History of the Scotch in North Carolina." 2 vols. Unpublished typewritten manuscript, North Carolina Archives, Raleigh, 1919. [Governor McLean secured the aid of several British researchers in preparing the material for this manuscript. Thus McLean is able to make lengthy quotations from the *Edinburgh Evening Courant*, *Edinburgh Adviser*, *Glasgow Journal*, and the *Caledonian Mercury*.]

Perry, Percival. "The Naval Stores Industry in the Ante-bellum South, 1789-1861." Unpublished doctoral dissertation, Duke University, Durham, N. C.

Books and Periodicals

Adam, Margaret I. "The Causes of the Highland Emigrations, 1783-1803," *Scottish Historical Review*, XVII (January, 1920), 73-89.

———. "Eighteenth Century Landlords and the Poverty Problem," *Scottish Historical Review*, XIX (October, 1921, and April, 1922), 1-20, 161-79.

———. "The Highland Emigration of 1770," *Scottish Historical Review*, XVI (July, 1919), 281-93.

Ashe, Samuel A'Court. *History of North Carolina.* Vol. I. Greensboro, N. C.: Charles L. Van Noppen, 1925.

Bain, Robert. *The Clans and Tartans of Scotland.* London: Collins, n.d.

Banks, James. *A Centennial Historical Address Delivered before the Presbytery of Fayetteville at the Bluff Church the 18th Day of October, 1858.* Fayetteville, N. C.: Presbyterian Office, 1858.

Bassett, John S. "The Influence of Coast Line and Rivers on North Carolina," *American Historical Association Annual Report, 1908*, I, 58-61.

Bingham, Edgar. *Physiographic Diagram of North Carolina.* New York: The Geographical Press, 1952.

Briggs, Charles A. *American Presbyterianism.* New York: Scribner's, 1885.

Brown, P. Hume. *History of Scotland.* 3 vols. University Press, Cambridge, 1909.

Browne, James. *The History of Scotland, Its Highlands, Regiments and Clans.* Vol. VI. Edinburgh: Francis A. Nicholls and Co., 1909.

Butler, Bion H. *Old Bethesda at the Head of Rockfish.* New York: Grosset & Dunlap, 1933.

The Cambridge Modern History, planned by Lord Acton, edited by A. W. Ward, *et al.* Vol. VI. New York: Macmillan Co., 1909.

Caruthers, Eli Washington. *Interesting Revolutionary Incidents: and Sketches of Character Chiefly in the Old North State.* Philadelphia: Hayes and Zell, 1856.

——. *Revolutionary Incidents: and Sketches of Character Chiefly in the Old North State.* Philadelphia: Hayes and Zell, 1854.

Connor, Robert D. W. *The History of North Carolina.* Vol. I. Chicago: Lewis Publishing Co., 1919.

——. *North Carolina: Rebuilding an Ancient Commonwealth, 1584-1925.* Vol. I. Chicago and New York: American Historical Society, Inc., 1929.

——. "Race Elements in the White Population of North Carolina," *North Carolina State Normal and Industrial College Historical Publications,* No. I (1920).

Corbitt, David Leroy. *The Formation of the North Carolina Counties, 1663-1943.* Raleigh: State Department of Archives and History, 1950.

Craig, David I. *History of the Development of the Presbyterian Church in North Carolina.* Richmond: Whittet, 1907.

Craighead, James G. *Scotch and Irish Seeds in American Soil.* Philadelphia: Presbyterian Board of Publications, 1878.

Crittenden, Charles C. *The Commerce of North Carolina, 1763-1789.* New Haven: Yale University Press, 1936.

Darrock, John. "The Scottish Highlanders Going to North Carolina," *The Celtic Magazine,* I (March, 1876), 142-47.

Davidson, Philip. *Propaganda and the American Revolution, 1763-1783.* Chapel Hill: University of North Carolina Press, 1941.

DeMond, Robert O. *The Loyalists in North Carolina During the Revolution.* Durham: Duke University Press, 1940.

Douglas, Ronald Macdonald. *The Scots Book.* New York: Macmillan Co., 1935.

Douglass, Elisha P. *Rebels and Democrats.* Chapel Hill: University of North Carolina Press, 1955.

Dunaway, Wayland F. *The Scotch-Irish in Colonial Pennsylvania.* Chapel Hill: University of North Carolina Press, 1944.

Dunn, Charles W. *Highland Settler: A Portrait of the Scottish Gael in Nova Scotia.* Toronto: University of Toronto Press, 1953.

Eardley-Simpson, Llewellyn. *Derby and the Forty-Five.* London: Phillip Allan, 1933.

Ergang, Robert. *Europe From the Renaissance to Waterloo.* Boston: D. C. Heath and Co., 1939.

Finley, John H. *The Coming of the Scot.* New York: Scribner's, 1940.

Foote, William Henry. *Sketches of North Carolina.* New York: Robert Carter, 1846.

Gipson, Lawrence Henry. *Great Britain and Ireland and the Southern Plantations.* ("The British Empire Before the American Revolution," Vols. I-II.) Caldwell, Idaho: Caxton Printers, Ltd., 1936.

Graham, Henry G. *The Social Life of Scotland in the Eighteenth Century.* London: A. and C. Black, Ltd., 1928.

Graham, Ian Charles Cargill. *Colonists from Scotland: Emigration to North America, 1707-1783.* Ithaca, N. Y.: Cornell University Press, 1956.

Grant, Isabel F. *Everyday Life on an Old Highland Farm, 1769-82.* London: Longmans, Green & Co., 1924.

Gray, Lewis C. *The History of Agriculture in the Southern United States to 1860.* 2 vols. Washington, D. C.: The Carnegie Institution of Washington, 1933.

Hanna, Charles A. *The Scotch-Irish.* Vol. II. New York: G. P. Putnam's Sons, 1902.

Harrell, Isaac S. "North Carolina Loyalists," *North Carolina Historical Review,* III (July, 1926), 575-89.

Harris, Marshall D. *Origin of the Land Tenure System in the United States.* Ames, Iowa: Iowa State College Press, 1953.

Hilldrup, R. L. "The Salt Supply of North Carolina During the American Revolution," *North Carolina Historical Review,* XXII (October, 1945), 393-417.

Hughson, Shirley Carter. "The Carolina Pirates and Colonial Commerce, 1670-1740," *Johns Hopkins University Studies,* Twelfth Series (1894), pp. 1-134.

Hydrologic Data on the Cape Fear River Basin, 1820-1945, ed. R. Bruce Etheridge. Washington: United States Geological Survey, 1947.

Insh, George P. *The Scottish Jacobite Movement: A Study in Economic and Social Forces.* Edinburgh: Moray Press, 1952.

Johnson, Guion G. *Ante-Bellum North Carolina.* Chapel Hill: University of North Carolina Press, 1937.

Johnson, Stanley C. *A History of Emigration: from the United Kingdom to North America, 1763-1912.* London: George Routledge & Sons, Ltd., 1913.

Lefler, Hugh Talmage and Albert Ray Newsome. *North Carolina: The History of a Southern State.* Chapel Hill: University of North Carolina Press, 1954.

MacDonald, Allan R. *The Truth about Flora MacDonald,* ed. Donald MacKinnon. Inverness: The Northern Chronicle Office, 1938.

MacDonald, Donald Farquard. *Scotland's Shifting Population, 1770-1850.* Glasgow: Jackson, Son & Co., 1937.

Mackinzie, Agnes Mure. *Scotland in Modern Times, 1720-1939.* London: W. & R. C. Chambers, Ltd., 1941.

Mackenzie, Alexander, *History of the Highland Clearances.* Glasgow: Alexander Maclaren & Sons, n.d.

Mackie, R. L. *Scotland.* London: George G. Harrap and Co., 1916.

MacLean, John P. *An Historical Account of the Settlements of Scotch Highlanders in America Prior to the Peace of 1783.* Cleveland: Helman-Taylor Co., 1900.

Macleod, Roderick C. "The Western Highlands in the Eighteenth Century," *Scottish Historical Review,* XIX (October, 1921), 33-48.

MacRae, James C. "The Highland-Scotch Settlement in North Carolina," *North Carolina Booklet,* IV (February, 1905).

Martin, Francois-Xavier. *The History of North Carolina from the Earliest Period.* 2 vols. New Orleans: A. T. Penneman, 1829.

McInnis, Edgar. *Canada: A Political and Social History.* New York: Rinehart and Company Inc., 1947.

McKay, Neill. *A Centenary Sermon Delivered Before the Presbytery of Fayetteville at Bluff Church, the 18th Day of October, 1858.* Fayetteville, N. C.: Presbyterian Office, 1858.

Notestein, Wallace. *The Scot in History.* New Haven: Yale University Press, 1947.

Oates, John A. *The Story of Fayetteville and the Upper Cape Fear.* Fayetteville, N. C.: the author, 1950.

Osgood, Herbert L. *The American Colonies in the Eighteenth Century.* Vol. II. New York: Columbia University Press, 1924.

Petrie, Charles A. *The Jacobite Movement: the Last Phase, 1716-1807.* London: Eyre & Spotteswoode, 1950.

Quynn, Dorothy Mackay. "Flora MacDonald in History," *North Carolina Historical Review,* XVIII (July, 1941), pp. 236-58.

Rait, Robert S. *The Making of Scotland.* London: A. and C. Black, Ltd., 1929.

Rankin, Hugh F. "The Moore's Creek Bridge Campaign, 1776," *North Carolina Historical Review,* XXX (January, 1953), 23.

Raper, Charles L. *North Carolina: A Study in English Colonial Government.* New York: Macmillan Co., 1904.

Ross, Peter. *The Scot in America.* New York: Raeburn Book Co., 1896.

Scott, Sir Walter. *Rob Roy. (Waverley Novels,* Vol. IV.) New York: Collier Publisher, n.d.

———. *Waverley.* Philadelphia: Porter and Coates, n.d.

Sikes, Enoch Walter. "North Carolina a Royal Province, 1729-1776," *The South in the Building of the Nation.* Vol. I. Richmond: Southern Historical Publication Society, 1909.

Sinclair, John C. "The Gaelic Element in North Carolina," *University of North Carolina Magazine,* X (November, 1860).

Smith, Abbott Emerson. *Colonists in Bondage: White Servitude and Convict Labor in America, 1607-1776.* Chapel Hill: University of North Carolina Press, 1947.

Stevenson, Robert L. *Kidnapped.* Chicago: Scott, Foresman & Co., 1921.

Taylor, Rosser Howard. *Slaveholding in North Carolina: an Economic View.* ("James Sprunt Historical Studies," Vol. XVIII.) Chapel Hill: University of North Carolina Press, 1926.

Trevelyan, George M. *English Social History.* London: Longmans, Green and Co., 1942.

Trinterud, Leonard J. *The Forming of an American Tradi-*

tion: a Re-examination of Colonial Presbyterianism.
Philadelphia: Westminster Press, 1949.

Van Tyne, Claude H. *The War of Independence, American Phase.* Boston and New York: Houghton Mifflin Co., 1929.

Webster, Richard. *A History of the Presbyterian Church in America.* Philadelphia: Joseph Wilson, 1857.

Wertenbaker, Thomas J. "Early Scotch Contributions to the United States," *Glasgow University Publications*, No. 64 (1945), pp. 8-10.

———. *The Old South.* New York: Scribner's, 1942.

Wheeler, John H. *Historical Sketches of North Carolina to 1851.* 2 vols. Philadelphia: Lippincott, Grambo & Co., 1851.

Williams, Basil. *The Whig Supremacy, 1714-1760.* Oxford: Clarendon Press, 1949.

Williamson, Hugh. *History of North Carolina.* 2 vols. Philadelphia: Thomas Dobson, 1812.

Wittke, Carl. *A History of Canada.* New York: Alfred A. Knopf, 1928.

Wrong, George M. *Canada and the American Revolution.* New York: Macmillan Co., 1935.

INDEX